Will You Answer the Call to Pray?

Will You Answer the Call to Pray?
Copyright © 2016 by Rev. Sandy Mays
Cover design by JHM Design Group

$\wp$

S-E-L-F PUBLISHING

Simple-Effective-Literary-Focusing on Publishing
10120 W. Flamingo Rd.
Suite 4 #228
Las Vegas, NV 89147

Visit us at www.yourpublisher.org

Printed in the United States of America.

Will You Answer the Call to Pray?

REVEREND SANDY MAYS

ℱ

S-E-L-F PUBLISHING

Simple- Effective-Literary-Focusing on Publishing

"Father, I'm teaming up with You,
to create Your will in my life
and in the world."

Matthew 12:35-37

DEDICATION

This book is dedicated to the furtherance of the Gospel of Jesus Christ and to the strengthening of the Body of Christ.

"And this is the confidence that we have in Him, that if we ask anything according to His will, He heareth us; and if we know that He heareth us, whatsoever we ask, we know that we have the petitions that we desired of Him."

1John 5:14-15 KJV

ACKNOWLEDGEMENT

To my wonderful daughter Jasmine and all of the members of "Las Vegas Church of the Harvest."

May this prayer guide establish you in power, love, the Anointing, and the Blessing of our Father God. I pray that your relationship with Him will flourish all the days of your life, and that you will walk in the perfect will of God on this earth, in the Name of Jesus.

TABLE OF CONTENTS

Lord, Let Your Word Be Planted And Rooted Firmly In My Heart Forevermore...

Ephesians 2:6 (AMP)
[6] *And He raised us up together with Him and made us sit down together [giving us joint seating with Him] in the heavenly sphere [by virtue of our being] in Christ Jesus (the Messiah, the Anointed One).*

God is a Good God

and

His Word is Truth

PRAYER OF SALVATION & BAPTISM OF THE HOLY SPIRIT

SALVATION PROMISE

Romans 10:9-10 (AMP)

⁹ Because if you acknowledge and confess with your lips that Jesus is Lord and in your heart believe (adhere to, trust in, and rely on the truth) that God raised Him from the dead, you will be saved.

¹⁰ For with the heart a person believes (adheres to, trusts in, and relies on Christ) and so is justified (declared righteous, acceptable to God), and with the mouth he confesses (declares openly and speaks out freely his faith) and confirms [his] salvation.

CONFESSION

God, according to Roman 10:9, I acknowledge and confess with my lips that Jesus is Lord and in my heart I believe (adhere to, trust in and rely on the truth) that You raised Him from the dead. Now I believe that I am saved, in the Name of Jesus.

THE HOLY SPIRIT PROMISE

Luke 11:11-13 (AMP)

¹¹ What father among you, if his son asks for a loaf of bread, will give him a stone; or if he asks for a fish, will instead of a fish give Him a serpent?

¹² Or if he asks for an egg, will give him a scorpion?

¹³ If you then, evil as you are, know how to give good gifts [gifts that are to their advantage] to your children, how much more will your heavenly Father give the Holy Spirit to those who ask and continue to ask Him!

Acts 2:4 (AMP)

⁴ And they were all filled (diffused throughout their souls) with the Holy Spirit and began to speak in other (different, foreign) language (tongues), as the Spirit kept giving them clear and loud expression in each tongue in appropriate words.

CONFESSION

Father, according to Luke 11:13 and Acts 2:4, I ask for the Gift of the Holy Spirit, with the evidence of speaking in other tongues. I believe I receive the Gift and I yield my mouth and my voice to the Holy Spirit. I now pray in other tongues, in the Name of Jesus.

INTRODUCTION

This is a Daily Guide for praying effectively according to God's Word. *God has commanded us to pray for kings and all those in authority that we may lead a quiet and peaceable life in all godliness and honesty (I Tim. 2:1-4).* This prayer outline will enable you to incorporate this command in your life and still cover the prayer needs for your family, friends and yourself. You will also learn how to pray the Word of God and receive His Promises by faith.

Daily dedication to prayer according to this guide, will bring a drastic change in your life and in the results you receive in answered prayer for yourself and others.

If you have not maintained a consistent prayer life, start by setting aside five minutes daily (preferably first thing in the morning). God will begin to increase your prayer time supernaturally. Before you know it you will be consistently praying an hour or more daily, receiving all the benefits of daily communion and fellowship with our Father God.

Remember, consistency is the key to success and to the power of God! (Quote from Gloria Copeland)

I Love you in Christ,

Pastor Sandy

Note: If you have been filled with the Holy Spirit and pray with other tongues, make sure to pray in the Spirit (in other tongues) in between each section. We must learn to rely on the Holy Spirit to increase our accuracy during prayer (Romans 8:26).

CREATIVE WAYS TO USE THIS PRAYER GUIDE

The object of *"Will You Answer the Call to Pray?"* is to enhance your prayer life through consistency and praying the Word of God. By praying the Word of God, we are saying what God says about us and creating God's vision for our lives. Developing your prayer life with these two ingredients will increase your faith, renew your mind, and tap you into the great power that God has made available for you. You will also experience the Grace of God to accomplish the will of God in your life. The power of God's Grace comes through faith and faith comes by hearing and hearing the Word of God (Roman 10:17).

There are many different ways to make this prayer guide accommodate your busy schedule such as:

1. Divide the book into sections and pray a different section each day;
2. Color code the sections of "Personalized Prayers For Every Area" so that you pray two or three different areas daily or weekly;
3. Take it with you and pray the whole guide throughout the day during breakfast, breaks, lunch and dinner.

Whatever way you are led by the Lord to start using it, let this prayer guide assist you in praying more effectively and consistently. We recommend praying in other tongues in between sections and the prewritten Scriptures. The Holy Spirit will enlighten your understanding and fill you with revelation knowledge as you allow Him to work in you while praying in other tongues.

There is no specific right way or wrong way to make it work for you. So just plunge right in and use your creativity!

Prophetic Word of the Lord
July 14, 2002
Given to Pastor Sandy Mays

"For there is a place," says the Lord, "that I have prepared just for you," says God. "There is a place in which you stand, oh, where you are protected," says the Lord, "where no foe can oppose or oppress you," says God. "But you must stand in that place," says the Lord.

"Oh, you must seek for that place everyday," says God. "For there is where My provision is for you, there is where My blessing is for you, there is where My presence is. Oh and everywhere that you go, My presence shall accompany you," says the Lord, "but you must stand in that place," says the Lord.

"Oh, you must daily rise up and decree, that you are standing in the place that I have prepared, that I predestined for you to stand in," says the Lord. "For there is safety, there is provision, there is strength, there is peace, there is joy, there is healing, for you in this place" says the Lord.

"Oh, so press into Me," says God, "press in with your whole heart and hold nothing back. Surrender what I have commanded you to surrender," says the Lord. "Put it down and let it go, for I call you this day to that place that I've prepared."

"I call you to stand in Me," says God "and in My power, for there is much work ahead, there is much to be done," says the Lord. "Oh, but stand in that place," says God and "surely, you shall see Me and you shall see My power," says God."

The Blood of Jesus

Will Never Lose

It's Power!

Come Into His Presence With Praise

Psalm 147:1 (AMP)
[1] PRAISE THE Lord! For it is good to sing praises to our God, for He is gracious and lovely; praise is becoming and appropriate.

Psalm 147:7 (AMP)
[7] Sing to the Lord with thanksgiving; sing praises with the harp or the lyre to our God!

PRAISE & WORSHIP THE LORD. BEGIN YOUR TIME WITH THE LORD WITH PRAISE AND THANKSGIVING TO HIM. COME BEFORE THE LORD, WITH AN ATTITUDE OF GRATITUDE.

WHY?
- When we praise God, He comes on the scene and Satan flees!
- Praise is the highest expression of faith.
- Every good thing in your life is from your Father God.

PRAISE HIM FOR:
- Praise Him for Who He is, the Most High God.
- Thank Him for His goodness to you.
- Thank Him for keeping you safe throughout the night.
- Praise Him for He has prepared and provided for you.
- Thank Him for having all of your faculties in order.
- Praise Him for His loving kindness and tender mercies in your life.

Father I Praise You for...

_____

_____

_____

_____

CONFESSION AND REPENTANCE OF SIN

1 John 1:9 (AMP)

[9] *If we [freely] admit that we have sinned and confess our sins, He is faithful and just (true to His own nature and promises) and will forgive our sins [dismiss our lawlessness] and [continuously] cleanse us from all unrighteousness [everything not in conformity to His will in purpose, thought, and action].*

I APPLY THE BLOOD OF JESUS OVER MY LIFE

CONFESSION

A. Father, in the Name of Jesus, I ask You to forgive me of my sins, mistakes, and trespasses?

1. I confess every sin and receive the mercy and atonement of the Blood of Jesus that has purged away every sin and its penalties from my life.

2. I receive the secure pardon from the penalties of sin on my life, so the Blessing of the Lord, now rests on me forever.

3. I plead the protection of the Blood of Jesus over my life, family, home, and every inch of my property. I decree the Blood line over every door and window of my home and declare, "NO EVIL WILL CROSS THAT BLOOD LINE," in the Name of Jesus.

4. I receive the liberty to hear Your voice and walk with You forever. I am sensitive to Your voice and every decision I make is in agreement with You.

5. I am conscious and sensitive to the righteousness You have given me.

B. Now the Blessing of the Lord is governing and abundantly increasing everything I do, without hindrances.

C. No good thing is delayed, stolen, or being withheld from me, in the Name of Jesus. That includes:

    1. My ministry, business, all the works of my hands, my relationships, every business appointment, every decision made about me, and every decision that I make.

    2. The curse has no place anywhere in my life, body, family, business ventures, or finances.

    3. By the protection of the Blood of Jesus, everything is secure here on earth, as it is in Heaven, in the Name of Jesus.

No Word Of God Will Ever Return To Him Void.

Preparing to Reign From His Right Hand

- Putting on the Whole Armor of God
- Yielding to the Ministry of the Holy Spirit
- Prayer for Wisdom and Revelation
- Taking my Seat at God's Right Hand

PUT ON THE WHOLE ARMOR OF GOD

Ephesians 6:10-18 (KJV)
[10] *Finally, my brethren, be strong in the Lord, and in the power of his might.*
[11] *Put on the whole armor of God, that ye may be able to stand against the wiles of the devil.*
[12] *For we wrestle not against flesh and blood, but against principalities, against powers, against the rulers of the darkness of this world, against spiritual wickedness in high places.*
[13] *Wherefore take unto you the whole armor of God, that ye may be able to withstand in the evil day, and having done all, to stand.*
[14] *Stand therefore, having your loins girt about with truth, and having on the breastplate of righteousness;*
[15] *And your feet shod with the preparation of the gospel of peace;*
[16] *Above all, taking the shield of faith, wherewith ye shall be able to quench all the fiery darts of the wicked.*
[17] *And take the helmet of salvation, and the sword of the Spirit, which is the word of God:*
[18] *Praying always with all prayer and supplication in the Spirit, and watching thereunto with all perseverance and supplication for all saints.*

CONFESSION

In the Name of Jesus, I put on the whole armor of God today, so that I may be able to stand against the wiles of the devil. For I wrestle not against flesh and blood, but against principalities, against powers, against the rulers of the darkness of this world, against spiritual wickedness in high places.

• I stand therefore, with my loins girded about with truth;

• I put on the breastplate of righteousness;

• I shod my feet with the preparation of the Gospel of peace;

- Above all, I take the shield of faith, wherewith I quench all the fiery darts of the wicked;

- I take the helmet of salvation;

- I take the sword of the Spirit, which is the Word of God (in my mouth);

- I pray always with all prayer and supplication in the spirit, as I watch with all perseverance and supplication for all the saints, in the Name of Jesus.

- The glory of the Lord is my rear guard (Isa. 58:8).

PRAY IN THE HOLY SPIRIT

1 Corinthians 14:2 (AMP)
For one who speaks in an [unknown] tongue speaks not to men but to God, for no one understands or catches his meaning, because in the [Holy] Spirit he utters secret truths and hidden things [not obvious to the understanding].

Begin to pray in your Heavenly language now and follow the unction of the Holy Spirit, as you continue praying through the following sections of this prayer guide.

PREPARING TO REIGN FROM HIS RIGHT HAND

John 16:13-15 (AMP)

[13] But when He, the Spirit of Truth (the Truth-giving Spirit) comes, He will guide you into all the Truth (the whole, full Truth). For He will not speak His own message [on His own authority]; but He will tell whatever He hears [from the Father; He will give the message that has been given to Him], and He will announce and declare to you the things that are to come [that will happen in the future].
[14] He will honor and glorify Me, because He will take of (receive, draw upon) what is Mine and will reveal (declare, disclose, transmit) it to you. [15] Everything that the Father has is Mine. That is what I meant when I said that He [the Spirit] will take the things that are Mine and will reveal (declare, disclose, transmit) it to you.

Romans 8:15-17 (KJV)

[15] For ye have not received the spirit of bondage again to fear; but ye have received the Spirit of adoption, whereby we cry, Abba, Father. [16] The Spirit itself beareth witness with our spirit, that we are the children of God: [17] And if children, then heirs; heirs of God, and joint-heirs with Christ; if so be that we suffer with him, that we may be also glorified together.

YIELDING TO THE MINISTRY OF THE HOLY SPIRIT

CONFESSION

1. Father, thank You for the ministry of the Holy Spirit. I surrender this time of prayer to the guidance and unction of the Holy Spirit, as He reveals, transmits, and discloses Your Truth to me, in the Name of Jesus.

2. I am sensitive to the transmission of Your Love, Light, and Life, that the Holy Spirit is filling within me.

3. The Holy Spirit is quickening me as I pray, bearing witness with my spirit that I am Your child and heir. The Holy Spirit is revealing to me all the riches of the glory of Your inheritance that is within me.

4. As I pray, the Holy Spirit is releasing the mysteries, of Your wisdom and power into the earth. Father, Your Kingdom is manifesting and You are being glorified, in the Name of Jesus.

5. I decree I am led today by the Holy Spirit into all Truth, mortifying the deeds of the flesh. I cry, "Abba Father" You are my Father and I am living my life as a Son (child), loved by You, Almighty God, in the Name of Jesus.

PRAYER FOR WISDOM AND REVELATION

CONFESSION

Ephesians 1:17-23 (KJV)

Father, I thank You, the God of our Lord Jesus Christ, the Father of glory, for giving unto me the Spirit of wisdom and revelation in the knowledge of You. The eyes of my understanding are being enlightened; so I know what is the hope of Your calling, and what the riches of the glory of Your inheritance is in me and the saints. Thank You, Father, for causing me to know what is the exceeding greatness of Your power towards me as a believer, according to the working of Your mighty power. Which You wrought in Christ, when You raised Him from the dead, and set Him [and me] at Your own Right Hand in the heavenly places, far above all principality, power, might, and dominion, and every name that is named, not only in this world, but also in that which is to come: And You hath put all things under His feet, [and under my feet] and gave Him to be the head over all things to the Church, which is his body, the fullness of him that filleth all in all, in the Name of Jesus.

1 John 3:23 (AMP)

Father, I submit to Your order (Your command, Your injunction): I believe in (put my faith and trust in and adhere to and rely on) the name of Your Son, Jesus Christ (the Messiah). and to love others, just as You have commanded me to, in the Name of Jesus.

1 Corinthians 6:17 (AMP)
But the person who is united to the Lord
becomes one spirit with Him.

Meditation:

I am united to the Lord and I have become
one spirit with Him. The same resurrection life
that flows in Him is flowing in me, in the
Name of Jesus.

The Word Of God Is the Power Of God Unto Salvation.

Taking My Seat At God's Right Hand

- I Believe I Sit Together In Christ in the Heavenlies
- As I Walk in the Spirit My Normal Life Is Reigning in the Heavenlies

Taking My Seat At God's Right Hand

CONFESSION
- God raised Jesus to His Right Hand.
- Jesus is the Head of the Body.
- God raised His Head and He raised His body.
- I am in His Body.

I Believe I sit together in Christ in the Heavenlies.

CONFESSION
A. Father, in humble faith, I do now take my place in the Heavenlies, in Christ Jesus, at Your Right Hand.

   1. Teach me how to fulfill this sacred ministry today; my ministry in the Heavenlies.

   2. Teach me how to exercise the authority that You have entrusted to me.

   3. Train me day by day, that I may attain to the full stature of the perfect man in Christ so that in me, Your purpose of the ages may be fulfilled.

As I walk in the Spirit my normal life Is Reigning in the Heavenlies.

B. To secure the consciousness that my life is reigning from the Heavenlies, there must be a daily acceptance of that fact.

CONFESSION
C. Morning by morning, my first act of worship to You, Father, is to take my seat with Christ, at Your Right Hand. Father, I thank You for all that this implies.

D. Today, I remind myself that I am seated far above all the powers of the air. They are in subjection to me and I am not in subjection to them, in the Name of Jesus.

E. My faith is learning day by day to use the Name and Authority of the Lord Jesus Christ.

    1. I am finding the spiritual forces yielding obedience in ways that are surprising me.

    2. All the spiritual laws of life are operating for me and the law of sin and death does not touch me or my family, in the Name of Jesus.

F. I am continuing to abide closely in You, and my prayers for the advancement of the Kingdom are becoming less and less the utterance of petitions.

G. My prayers for the Kingdom are increasing and I exercise a spiritual authority that recognizes no natural boundaries.

H. I am fearlessly binding the forces of darkness in every part of the world.

I. I am a king and priest of You Father, the Almighty God. I am acting in Your Authority and there is no authority greater, in the Name of Jesus.

J. I decree, greater is He Who is in me, than he who is in the world, in the Name of Jesus. [1John 4:4 BBE]

Content of this section taken from Page 27 of "The Authority of the Believer" by John A McMillian, Revised Edition by Billye Brim Ministries PO Box 40 Branson, MO 6561

CONFESSION

Romans 5:17 (AMP) Father, it is written that, because of one man's trespass (lapse, offense) death reigned through that one, much more surely because I receive [Your] overflowing grace (unmerited favor) and the free gift of righteousness which has [put me into right standing with You], I am reigning as a king in life through the One Man Jesus Christ (the Messiah, the Anointed One), in the Name of Jesus.

Ephesians 2:1 (KJV) Father, You have quickened me, when I was dead in trespasses and sins, in the Name of Jesus.

Ephesians 2:4-6 (AMP) Father, thank You, for the richness of your mercy! Because of and in order to satisfy the great and wonderful and intense love with which You loved me, (Your favor and mercy which I did not deserve) I have been saved (delivered from judgment and made a partaker of Christ's salvation). Even when I was dead, (slain) by [my own] shortcomings and trespasses, You made me alive together in fellowship and in union with Christ; [You gave me the very life of Christ Himself, the same new life with which You quickened Him], for it is by grace; (Your favor and mercy which I did not deserve) that I have been saved (delivered from judgment and made a partaker of Christ's salvation). And You raised me up together with Him and made me sit down together [giving me joint seating with Him] in the heavenly sphere [by virtue of my being] in Christ Jesus (the Messiah, the Anointed One).

Revelation 1:5-6 (KJV) Father, I give glory to Your Name for Jesus Christ, Who is the faithful witness, and the first begotten of the dead, and the prince of my life as a king of the earth. Unto You, Who has loved me, and washed me from my sins, in His [Jesus Christ's] his own blood, You have made me a king and a priest unto You; God and His Father. To You be glory and dominion for ever and ever, in the Name of Jesus.

The Name Of Jesus Has All Rule and Authority Over Every Name.

Reigning From His Right Hand

- Exercising Dominion and Authority Over the Earth
- Bind Satan and the Kingdom of Darkness
- Enforcing Divine Protection
- Pray in the Holy Spirit

REIGNING FROM HIS RIGHT HAND

EXERCISING DOMINION AND AUTHORITY OVER THE EARTH

CONFESSION

Father, I am here at Your Right Hand to bring You glory. Thank You for Your great plan of redemption, and for seating me here at Your Right Hand, through the Blood of Jesus. In order to bring You glory, You told me to reign in this life as a king, so I am going to reign over Satan and the kingdom of darkness, today. This is all for Your glory, in the Name of Jesus.

Father, as I sit here at Your Right Hand, I am clothed in the abundance of grace and the Gift of Righteousness. I reign over the earth, bringing all things into Your divine order and Authority, by the power of Your spoken Word.

A. I reign and rule over the earth, the nations, my state, my city, and my neighborhood.

B. In the Name of Jesus, by the power of the Blessing, I master and rule over:
    - Time
    - The Soil and Products of the Earth
    - The Fruits of the trees
    - The Communication Systems and Media
    - The Wealth of the Earth (financial institutions and systems)
    - Everything that creeps on the earth
    - The Power Supplies (all the resources of the earth)
    - The Real Estate and lands
    - The Airways
    - The Economy
    - Nature and the Weather

Confession

I release the power of the Blessing of the Lord to cause all the works of my hands to be fruitful, multiply, thrive, and replenish the earth with the glory of the Lord, in the Name of Jesus.

By the power of the Blessing of the Lord, this city _____ and all the earth is yielding forth my increase into my hands, in the Name of Jesus.

2 Peter 1:3-4 (AMP) Father, I receive the divine power that You have bestowed upon me, giving me all things that [are requisite and suited] to life and godliness, through the [full, personal] knowledge of You. You have called me by and to Your own glory and excellence (virtue). By this You have bestowed on me Your precious and exceedingly great promises. Now I have escaped [by flight] from the moral decay (rottenness and corruption) that is in the world because of covetousness (lust and greed). Now I am sharing (partaking) of Your divine nature, in the Name of Jesus.

Mark 11:24 (BBE) Praise God, whenever I make a request in prayer, I have faith that it has been given to me at that very moment. I possess it, mastering over time as I take it with my faith. My faith giving expression and reality to it, from that moment on, in the Name of Jesus.

I believe I receive when I pray, therefore, I am mastering over time all for the glory of God, in the Name of Jesus.

BIND SATAN AND THE KINGDOMS OF DARKNESS

1John 5:18 (AMP)
[18] *We know [absolutely] that anyone born of God does not [deliberately and knowingly] practice committing sin, but the One Who is begotten of God carefully watches over and protects him [Christ's divine presence within him preserves him against the evil], and the wicked one does not lay hold (get a grip) on him or touch [him].*

Colossians 1:13 (AMP)
[13] *[The Father] has delivered and drawn us to Himself out of the control and the dominion of darkness and has transferred us into the kingdom of the Son of His love.*

CONFESSION

Father, I am here at Your Right Hand, answering Your call to reign in life as a king for Your glory, in the Name of Jesus. Satan and kingdoms of darkness, you listen to me, it is written that I am seated at the Right Hand of the Father and I am here to put limits on you today. I plead the Blood of Jesus over my life and my family. It is written that I overcome you by the Blood of Jesus and the word of my testimony, so I decree the Blood of Jesus around all the good works that God has ordained for me and my family to walk in. We are born of God, and our lives are carefully watched over and protected by Christ's divine presence. I decree the wicked one does not lay hold of us, in the Jesus Name.

OUR AUTHORITY

CONFESSION

Colossians 2:15 (AMP) Father, You have disarmed the principalities and powers that were ranged against us and made a bold display and public example of them, by triumphing over them in Him and in it [the cross], in the Name of Jesus.

Luke 10:19 (KJV) Thank You Father, for giving me authority to tread upon serpents and scorpions and over all the power of the enemy. Nothing shall hurt me or my family, in the Name of Jesus.

Matthew 16:19 (KJV) Father, I give glory to Your name, for You have given me the keys of the kingdom of heaven and whatsoever I bind on earth shall be bound in heaven and whatsoever I loose on earth shall be loosed in Heaven, in the Name of Jesus.

Matthew 10:1 (KJV) Father, just as Jesus gave to His twelve disciples, power and authority over unclean spirits, I receive that same power and authority also. I use it to drive out unclean spirit and to cure all kinds of diseases and all kinds of weakness and infirmities, in the Name of Jesus. (For more prayers see "Authority in the Name of Jesus" section, page 91.)

ENFORCE SATAN'S DEFEAT

CONFESSION
Matthew 18:18 (KJV) Satan, in the Name of Jesus, I bind you and all the kingdoms of darkness from my life and from my family and our affairs. You have no part in our lives anywhere. I enforce your defeat and I stand in mastery and authority over you. I loose all our inheritance and the fullness of our restoration and mega harvest of the earth, to come into our hands now. You will no longer withhold from us. You are beneath our feet and now we are treading over you and over all your power, in the Name of Jesus.

DISPATCH YOUR ANGELS

CONFESSION
Psalm 103:20 (KJV) Angels I employ and command you in behalf of myself and my family to do our bidding. Carry out God's plans for our lives and bring our mega harvest into our hands now, according to the Word of God, in the Name of Jesus.

ENFORCING DIVINE PROTECTION

CONFESSION

Psalm 91 (KJV) My family and I live in the shelter of the Most High and we are lodged under the shadow of the Almighty. I say, "The Lord is our safe retreat, our God the fastness in which we trust. He Himself is snatching us away from the fowler's snare and raging tempest. He is covering us with His pinions (feathers), and we are finding safety beneath His wings. God's truth is our shield and our rampart. We don't fear the hunters' trap by night or the arrow that flies by day, the pestilence that stalks in the darkness nor the plague raging at noonday. A thousand may fall at our side, and ten thousand close at hand, but it shall not touch us. With our eyes we see all this, as we watch the punishment of the wicked. The Lord is our safe retreat; we have made the most high our refuge. [No disaster shall befall us: no terrorist, terrorism, sickness, affliction, terminal illnesses, cancers, diseases, sudden death, poverty, lack, prejudice, racism, murderers, violators, lawless people, no thievery of my life, family or material possessions, no calamity, tragedy, or catastrophe shall come upon our home, bodies, or dwelling place.] The angels have charge over our lives; they guard us wherever we go, to lift us up in their hands for fear that we should strike our foot against a stone. We are stepping on the asp and cobra, treading safely on the snake and serpent. Because we have set our love on the Lord, He is delivering us and lifting us beyond danger, because we know His name. When we call upon Him, He is answering us and being with us in the time of trouble. He is rescuing us and bringing us to honor. He is satisfying us with long life to enjoy the fullness of His salvation, in the Name of Jesus.

Psalm 121:2-5 (AMP) Father, You are the maker of heaven and earth. I praise You, for You are our helper. I boldly say that our help comes from You Lord. Thank You for not allowing our foot to slip or to be moved, because You never sleep nor slumber. You are our keeper and our shade on our right side [the side not carrying a shield], in the Name of Jesus.

PRAY IN THE HOLY SPIRIT

Romans 8:26 (BBE)
[26] And in the same way the Spirit is a help to our feeble hearts: for we are not able to make prayer to God in the right way; but the Spirit puts our desires into words which are not in our power to say.

A. Pray in the Power of the Holy Spirit In Your Heavenly Language (Other Tongues).

    1. As we are seated at the Right Hand of the Father, praying in the power of the Holy Spirit over the earth, the Holy Spirit will give us divine utterance.

    2. While praying in our Heavenly language we are praying out the mysteries of God over the earth.

    3. The more we pray in our Heavenly language, the more sensitive we will become as we pray for our President, all governmental leaders, all issues in our nation and the world, including our families and lives.

Continue praying in your Heavenly language now and follow the Holy Spirit's unction as you continue praying through the following sections of this prayer guide.

CONFESSION

Romans 8:26 (BBE) Father, I am praying out all Your mysteries into the earth, I receive the help of the Holy Spirit to offer prayer to You in the right way, in the Name of Jesus.

Proverbs 20:27 (AMP)

The spirit of man [that factor in human personality which proceeds immediately from God] is the lamp of the Lord, searching all his innermost parts.

Meditation:

My spirit [the factor in my human personality which proceeds immediately from God] is the lamp of the Lord, searching all my innermost parts. He is revealing secrets, ideas, concepts, knowledge of witty invention, and giving me instructions and direction about my life within my spirit, in the Name of Jesus.

I Am A King and Priest Unto the Almighty God, in the Name of Jesus.

Reigning in Prayer From His Right Hand

- Pray for President and all Leaders
- Spiritual Leaders
- Pray for Our Nation's Protection
- Pray for the Peace of Jerusalem
- Pray for the Harvest
- Pray for Others
- Pray for Ministry and Business Associates
- Pray for Your Family

Reigning From His Right Hand

Pray For Our President and All Leaders

1 Tim. 2:1-4 (KJV)
[1] I exhort therefore, that, first of all, supplications, prayers, inter-cessions, and giving of thanks, be made for all men; [2] For kings, and for all that are in authority; that we may lead a quiet and peaceable life in all godliness and honesty. [3] For this is good and acceptable in the sight of God our Saviour; [4] Who will have all men to be saved, and to come unto the knowledge of the truth.

Confession
1 John 1:9 (KJV)   Father, I repent for the laws and ordinances that have been enacted, which are against Your will, plan, and purposes for this our nation. Thank You for forgiving us and putting the right people in every office of authority, in our nation, every state, and every city. I say by faith, that they are repealing every law and ordinance that is against You and Your Word. I believe that those currently in office, are only enacting the laws and ordi-nances that are in line with Your Word and Your will for the United States, in the Name of Jesus.

A. Executive, Legislative, Judicial, and Local Government
President of the United States; all National, State, and City Political Officials, the U.S. House and Senate, the Supreme Court, all Legislative Officials, Judiciaries, Political Staff, City Officials, and City Council persons.

   1. Father, in the Name of Jesus, I pray for the outpouring of the former and latter rain to flood our nation and pre-pare the hearts of all our leaders to receive and operate in line with the Truth of Your Word, in all matters con-cerning our government.

   2. I command all forces of darkness and evil to cease and

desist in all your maneuvers to control the leaders of this nation and all decisions being made.

3. I pray for revival of the Holy Spirit to impact all our government, nation and all our leaders.

4. I decree that only born again, Spirit-filled Christians fill the offices of authority of our government and nation.

5. I say by faith, that this nation has returned to the Biblical and Christian values that it was founded on. I plead the Blood of Jesus over those values and declare they are honored by all, in the Name of Jesus.

6. I pray for the restoration and prosperity of our nation's economy as we continue to carry the Gospel all over the World. Satan, take your hands off our economy and loose the financial prosperity of our nation.

7. I decree that all our leaders are leading our nation for the common good of all mankind, by the power of the Holy Spirit, in the Name of Jesus.

B. Praying For God's Will in Governmental Elections

1. Father, I pray that every member of the Body of Christ will take their responsibility to pray and seek Your Will before voting.

2. I declare that every Christian will vote according to Your leading, Father, and not according to what is socially or politically correct, in the Name of Jesus.

- Pray in your heavenly language (in other tongues) for our President and the United States.

Make a list of specific leaders and governmental issues needing prayer.

Father, in the Name of Jesus, I pray for...

_____

_____

_____

_____

_____

_____

_____

_____

_____

_____

_____

_____

_____

_____

_____

_____

_____

PRAY FOR INTERNATIONAL LEADERS

C. Governing Leaders of All Foreign Countries and Nations
Political, Appointed, and Monarchial Leaders

1. Father, in the Name of Jesus, I pray for an outpouring of the Holy Spirit to prepare the hearts of the leaders and the people in these countries to receive the teaching and preaching of the Word of God, and Jesus Christ as Lord.

2. I pray for the Lord of the harvest to send laborers to preach and teach the Word of God to the leaders and the people in all foreign nations.

3. I pray for the outpouring of the Holy Spirit to water every seed sown in the hearts of the leaders and the people, to bring the harvest of souls into the Kingdom of God, in the Name of Jesus.

4. I pray for the power of the Holy Spirit to influence all of the leaders to make their decisions in line with the will of God concerning international relations between their countries and the United States.

Make a list of specific leaders and governmental issues needing prayer.

Father, in the Name of Jesus, I pray for...

_____

_____

_____

_____

PRAY FOR SPIRITUAL LEADERS

D. Five-Fold Ministry Gifts
Apostles, Prophets, Evangelists, Pastors and Teachers

1. Father, in the Name of Jesus, I pray for the outpouring of the former and latter rain to flood the Church and to bring Your glory and the "Great Awakening" into every service.

2. I pray for unity of the Spirit and the bond of peace in love to dominate the lives of the leaders and members of the Body of Christ.

3. I declare that *great grace* is upon the five-fold ministry Gifts and that the Church is increasing in numbers by the multitudes.

4. I pray that the Spirit of the Lord would rest on them; the Spirit of wisdom and understanding, the Spirit of counsel, might, the Spirit of knowledge and of the reverential and obedient fear of the Lord.

5. I pray that the Anointing of the Holy Ghost and power will rest on the leaders and members of the Body of Christ, to preach and demonstrate the burden removing, yoke destroying Power of God.

6. I pray that no weapon formed against the Church will prosper and that God would enable them to confute every tongue that rises against them in judgment.

7. I pray for supernatural peace, provision and protection over all the leaders, missionaries and members of the Body of Christ, living in all foreign countries and nations.

Make a list of specific leaders and spiritual issues needing prayer.

Father, in the Name of Jesus, I pray for…

_____

_____

_____

_____

_____

_____

_____

_____

_____

_____

_____

_____

_____

_____

_____

_____

Pray For The Peace of Jerusalem

Psalm 122:6 (AMP)
⁶ Pray for the peace of Jerusalem! May they prosper who love you [the Holy City]!

E. The Peace and the Protection, of the Lord, is Covering Jerusalem.

1. Father, in the Name of Jesus, I pray for the outpouring of the Holy Spirit to water all the seeds of Your Word, that are being planted in the leaders and in all the people of the Jewish nations;

2. I pray that the "Great Awakening" is taking place by the power of the Holy Spirit; influencing, and compelling all of Jerusalem to accept the full knowledge of the Truth, that Jesus Christ is the Messiah;

3. I praise You Father God for protecting, defending, and preserving Jerusalem from their enemies and for causing Your wisdom to rest upon their Prime Minister and all leaders;

   a. I pray that no weapon formed against them will prosper;
   b. I pray that their enemies would be at peace with them forever;

4. I plead the Blood of Jesus over the alliance of peace between the United States and Jerusalem.

   a. I decree that it will never ever be severed, in the Name of Jesus.

Make a list of additional people, needs and issues needing prayer.

Father, in the Name of Jesus, I pray for…

PRAY FOR OUR NATION'S PROTECTION

Psalm 91:1-2 (AMP)

[1] He who dwells in the secret place of the Most High shall remain stable and fixed under the shadow of the Almighty [Whose power no foe can withstand]. [2] I will say of the Lord, He is my Refuge and my Fortress, my God; on Him I lean and rely, and in Him I [confidently] trust!

F. My Nation is Safe and Secure

1. Father, in the Name of Jesus, I declare that, The United States, my state, city, and my neighborhood are protected by the Blood of Jesus, hidden in the secret place of the Most High, and lodged under Your Shadow, Almighty God;

2. I pray that my nation would be a step ahead of all the powers of darkness at all times;

3. I pray that You would reveal and stop all terrorists: their plots, weapons, and locations to our nation's defense systems, military forces, and law enforcement agencies by the power of the Holy Spirit, according to the Promise of Daniel 2:29;

4. I pray the Spirit of Wisdom and Revelation would rest upon the CIA, FBI, and NSA, giving them supernatural wisdom to stop all acts and threats of terrorism;

5. I plead the Blood of Jesus over our water, food, power, and air supply, to enforce divine protection from the Hand of God. I decree all plans, strategies, and devices of attack, being prepared to be launched against our nation are destroyed, in the Name of Jesus.

Pray For Our Nation's Protection

7. I bind the spirit of fear, terrorism, racism, division, and hatred, from the United States and I loose the spirit of faith, courage, peace, love, and unity, in the Name of Jesus;

8. I bind all beheadings, massacres, bombings, weapons of mass destruction, nuclear, viral, and bacterial warfare, cyber attacks, attacks on our national grid, and natural disasters. I loose the authority of the Blood of Jesus to bring divine protection and intervention to stop every incident, in the Name of Jesus;

9. I plead the Blood of Jesus over the physical borders of our nation and our airspace;

10. I declare no harm can come to my city and I plead the Blood of Jesus over our:
    - Financial institutions
    - Communication systems
    - Cell towers
    - Transportation systems
    - Airports
    - Train & bus stations
    - Railroads, highways and interstates
    - Schools and colleges
    - Churches
    - Grocery stores, malls, and shopping centers
    - All other public venues

11. I plead the Blood of Jesus over the spirit, soul, and body of all our law enforcement, all military troops and all civil authorities. I decree they are God's servants for good.

I bind all forces of darkness from operating through them. I loose the power of the Holy Spirit upon them, to do the perfect will of God in every encounter of protecting our neighborhoods, cities, states, and nation, in the Name of Jesus. [Rom. 13:3-4]

Make a list of other specific locations, such as the name of your child's school, your workplace, etc.

Father, in the Name of Jesus, I pray for…

_____

_____

_____

_____

_____

_____

_____

_____

_____

_____

_____

Make a list of other specific locations, such as the name of your child's school, your workplace, etc.

Father, in the Name of Jesus, I pray for…

_____

_____

_____

_____

_____

_____

_____

_____

_____

_____

_____

_____

_____

_____

_____

_____

PRAY FOR THE HARVEST

Matthew 9:37-*38* (KJV)
[37]Then saith he unto his disciples, The harvest truly is plenteous, but the labourers are few; [38]Pray ye therefore the Lord of the harvest, that he will send forth labourers into his harvest.

G. The Unsaved and Backslidden
In my Neighborhood, City, State, Nation, and in all Foreign Countries and Nations.

1. Father, in the Name of Jesus, I pray for the outpouring of the Holy Spirit to prepare the hearts of all of humanity to receive the Word of God.

2. I pray for the Lord of the harvest to send laborers into every Gentile and Jewish nation, to teach them the Word of God.

3. I pray for the outpouring of the Holy Spirit to water the seeds of the Word of God that have been planted in the hearts of humanity, resulting in multitudes of people confessing Jesus Christ as their Lord, in the Name of Jesus.

4. I pray for the power, revelation and utterance gifts to enable the laborers to minister effectively, compelling the lost and the backslidden to come into the Body of Christ.

    a. I command the blinders to be removed from the eyes of the lost.

    b. I pray for God to grant Godly-sorrow to the backsliders, causing them to return to Jesus Christ.

5. Speak to the North, South, East, and West to give up the harvest, in the Name of Jesus.

Make a list of people to pray for in our nation and all over the world.

Father, in the Name of Jesus, I pray for...

_____

_____

_____

_____

_____

_____

_____

_____

_____

_____

_____

_____

_____

_____

PRAY FOR OTHERS

James 5:16 (AMP)
[16] *Confess to one another therefore your faults (your slips, your false steps, your offenses, your sins) and pray [also] for one another, that you may be healed and restored [to a spiritual tone of mind and heart]. The earnest (heartfelt, continued) prayer of a righteous man makes tremendous power available [dynamic in its working].*

Ephesians 4:12-13 (KJV)
[12] *For the perfecting of the saints, for the work of the ministry, for the edifying of the Christ* [13] *Till we all come in the unity of the faith, and of the knowledge of the Son of God, unto a perfect man, unto the measure of the stature of the* fullness of Christ.

H. **Members of the Body of Christ**

Praying for the members of your Church family and the Body of Christ is important for their growth and wellbeing, as well as your own. As we pray for each other we will establish unity, the bond of peace and love in the Body of Christ.

Make a list of people the Holy Spirit inspires you to pray for.

CONFESSION
Father, in the Name of Jesus, I pray that the Anointing will remove every burden, yoke, obstacle, and hindrance off of the lives of...

_____

_____

_____

_____

_____

Make a list of people the Holy Spirit inspires you to pray for.

Father, in the Name of Jesus, I pray for…

_____

_____

_____

_____

_____

_____

_____

_____

_____

_____

_____

_____

_____

_____

_____

_____

_____

PRAY FOR MINISTRY AND BUSINESS ASSOCIATES

Proverbs 15:29 (AMP)
[29] *The Lord is far from the wicked, but He hears the prayer of the [consistently] righteous (the upright, in right standing with Him).*

I. *My Ministry and Business Associates*

CONFESSION
Father, in the Name of Jesus, I plead the Blood of Jesus over all the members, volunteers, employees, business partners, advisors, investors, and supporters of _____ *(insert the name your ministry or business here).*

Satan and kingdoms of darkness, you will not deceive, hinder, or stop them from obeying the leading of the Holy Spirit concerning their role and call at _____ *(your ministry or business name).*

They are heeding the direction and instruction of God concerning their contribution to _____ *(your ministry or business name)* and together we operate in unity as one body, in the bond of peace and love. I bind offense, jealousy, envy, and strife from them and loose the love of God on them, in the Name of Jesus.

Make a list of specific associates to pray for.

Satan, in the Name of Jesus, you will stay away from...

_____

_____

_____

_____

Pray For Your Family

Acts 16:31 (AMP)
[31] And they answered, Believe in the Lord Jesus Christ [give yourself up to Him, take yourself out of your own keeping and entrust yourself into His keeping] and you will be saved, [and this applies both to] you and your household as well.

J. **My Family**
> *Spouse, Children, Grandchildren, Siblings, Relatives, In-laws and Close Friends*

Confession

Father, in the Name of Jesus, I plead the Blood of Jesus over my family members. Satan and kingdoms of darkness, you will not deceive, hinder, or touch my family, in the Name of Jesus. You get away and STAY AWAY FROM THEM, in the Name of Jesus. They are covered by the mercy, protection, power, and the Authority of the Blood of Jesus.

I plead the Blood of Jesus over every decision made about them, and every decision they make, and I declare that only the decisions in line with the plan, will, grace, and Blessing of the Lord, will prevail in their lives, in the Name of Jesus.

I declare that all my family members are reigning in the earth, as kings and priests of Almighty God. The wisdom and power of God is on them, in all that they do, and everywhere that they go.

Father, I praise You for granting to all of my family members, the Spirit of Wisdom and Revelation [of insight into mysteries and secrets] in the [deep and intimate] knowledge of You, by flooding the eyes of their hearts with light. Now they know *and* understand the hope to which You have called them, and they see the riches of Your glorious inheritance, in the saints (Your set-apart ones). I say by faith, that they are daily growing in knowledge and understanding of the immeasurable, unlimited, and surpassing greatness of Your power in and for them as believers, in the Name of Jesus.

The law of the Spirit of life [which is] in Christ Jesus, [the law of their new being], has freed them from the law of sin and death. Therefore, every cancer cell and free radical that comes near their bodies, dies instantly. Every terminal illness, sickness, and disease that comes near my family dies instantly, in the Name of Jesus. There are no mutant cells, free radicals, cancerous tumors, cysts, growths, masses, nodules, lesions, or lumps anywhere in their bodies. Their immune systems are protecting every part of their bodies. Every infection, plague, virus, bacteria, fungus, and germ that comes near them, I demand dies instantly. Sickness, disease and infirmities cannot live, bear fruit, or eat the fruit of their bodies, in the Name of Jesus.

My family members are glorifying God and their lives are not being stolen from them, nor are they being taken captive by any evil, in the Name of Jesus.

Make a list of your family members.

Father, in the Name of Jesus, I pray for…

_____

_____

_____

_____

_____

Make a list of your family members.

Father, in the Name of Jesus, I pray for...

Make a list of your family members.

Father, in the Name of Jesus, I pray for…

_____

_____

_____

_____

_____

_____

_____

_____

_____

_____

_____

_____

_____

_____

_____

_____

I Am Fulfilling the Call And Plan Of God For My Life, in the Name of Jesus.

Reigning From His Right Hand For Your Personal Life

- Put on the Anointing
- Plead the Blood of Jesus Over Your Spirit, Soul and Body
- Developing my Human Spirit
- Divine Health and Healing
- My Longevity
- Activating the Blessing of the Lord for Finances
- Reaping my Harvest
- Seedtime and Harvest
- Ready, Set & Go

Reigning From His Right Hand

For Your Personal Life

Put on the Anointing

Luke 4:18-19 (AMP) *(Written in first person present tense)*
[18] The Spirit of the Lord [is] upon Me, because He has anointed Me with the power of [the Anointed One, and the Anointing of the Messiah] to preach the good news (the Gospel) to the poor; He has sent Me to announce release to the captives and recovery of sight to the blind, to send forth as delivered those who are oppressed [who are downtrodden, bruised, crushed, and broken down by calamity], [19] I am here to proclaim the accepted and acceptable year of the Lord [the day when salvation and the free Favors, of God profusely abound], in the Name of Jesus.

CONFESSION

Father, I receive the Anointing with the Holy Spirit and power to preach and demonstrate the Gospel to the world; to do the same works that my Lord Jesus Christ did, all for Your glory. I am anointed, to be the best, to influence, compel and lead in everything that I do at a level the world is not familiar with, all for the glory of God.

I am anointed with divine health and healing, divine prosperity, divine insight and wisdom, divine ability, strength, grace, poise, and professionalism. My success and results are at a level this world is not familiar with all for the glory of God, in the Name of Jesus.

Plead the Blood of Jesus over your Spirit, Soul & Body

CONFESSION

I plead the Blood of Jesus over my spirit, soul, and body.
Satan and kingdoms of darkness, you will not deceive or touch me in any area of my life. The Blessing of the Lord, the Anointing of the Holy Ghost, and His power, is providing supernatural: wisdom, vision, discipline, abilities, and success in achieving my goals. My goals are: wealth, witty inventions, material goods, opportunities, and favor with the right people. I am operating from a level of power that the world is not familiar with, all for the glory of God. I am attaining the call and purpose of God for my life and I am not being taken captive by any evil, in the Name of Jesus.

I plead the Blood of Jesus around my mega harvest of the earth that is coming to me now. No good thing is being with-held from me, in the Name of Jesus.

Today my results are filled by:

- the right doors are opening up for me and doors of adversity and persecution are being closed, in Jesus Name;
- ownership of real estate for my ministry and business are being given to me now, in the Name of Jesus;
- people with expertise and talents are giving of their resources and abilities to help me fulfill the plan of God, in the Name of Jesus;
- the grace of God (ability, unmerited favor and opportunities) is abounding to me and through me so that things that seemed impossible are coming to pass daily, in the Name of Jesus;
- I am anointed with divine favor, wisdom, and influence to lead thousands of people, and I have surpassed the wisdom of my teachers, in the Name of Jesus.

Developing My Human Spirit

CONFESSION

John 6:63 (AMP) The Spirit is giving me life [He is the Life giver]. The Words of truth that He speaks to me are spirit and life. Every Word is filling me with Light and eternal life, in the Name of Jesus.

Romans 8:2 (NLT) I belong to God and the Life-giving Spirit has freed me from the power of sin that leads to death. My life is free from the wages of sin (sickness, disease and everything that is under the curse), in the Name of Jesus.

1 Thessalonians 5:23 (AMP) The God of all peace Himself has sanctified me through and through [separated me from profane things, made me pure and wholly consecrated me to Himself]. Thank You Father, for preserving my spirit, soul and body, wholly consecrated to You, I am preserved sound, complete and found blameless at the coming of our Lord Jesus Christ (the Messiah), in the Name of Jesus.

Romans 1:9 (AMP) I am a spirit and I serve God with my whole spirit [rendering priestly and spiritual service], while preaching the good news of the Gospel, in the Name of Jesus.

1 Peter 3:3-4 (NLT) Father, I clothe myself with the beauty that comes from within me (the beauty of my recreated spirit, born of You). My outward beauty is secondary to my inward beauty. I am living my life by the unfading beauty of a gentle and quiet spirit, which is so precious to You. My outward beauty is perfect because of the inward perfect beauty that is shining through me, in the Name of Jesus.

CONFESSION

John 1:4-5 (NLT) Glory to God, the Word has given life to me and His life is giving light to me. Now His light is my light and it is shining in the darkness and the darkness in the world can not extinguish it, in the Name of Jesus.

Daniel 1:17 (NLT) God is giving me unusual aptitude for understanding every aspect of literature and wisdom. I am ten times smarter than my peers. And God has given me special ability to interpret the meanings of visions and dreams, in the Name of Jesus.

Divine Health & Healing

CONFESSION

Isaiah 53:5 (AMP) But Jesus was wounded for my transgressions, He was bruised for my guilt *and* iniquities; the chastisement need- ful to obtain] peace *and* well-being for me was upon Him, and with the stripes [that wounded] Him I am are healed and made whole. [I have no terminal illnesses, sicknesses, or diseases anywhere in my body and I am in perfect chemical, hormonal, and electrical balance], in the Name of Jesus.

1 Corinthians 11:15 (KJV) Thank You Father, for blessing me with long, thick, shiny beautiful hair. [It is not breaking, thinning, shedding, receding, balding, or prematurely graying]. It is an orna- ment of glory for my covering, in the Name of Jesus.

Jeremiah 33:6 (AMP) Father, I thank You for laying upon me health and healing, and curing me and revealing to me and my family Your abundance of peace (prosperity, security, stability) and truth, in the Name of Jesus.

Proverbs 18:21 (KJV) Praise God, death and life are in the power of my tongue. I am keeping my mouth full of the Word of God, speaking life, peace, healing, tranquility, preservation to every sys- tem, and organ in my body. I am eating the fruit of speaking the Words of Life, in the Name of Jesus.

CONFESSION

I plead the Blood of Jesus over my whole spirit, soul, and body. The Anointing is preserving my health from all sickness, disease, abnormalities, distresses, and premature aging, at a level of life and strength this world and medical science is not familiar with. I am anointed of God to live out the fullness of my days, up to 120 years, in divine health and peace with a strong sound mind, all for the glory of God, in the Name of Jesus.

Romans 8:2 (AMP) Praise God, the law of the Spirit of life [which is] in Christ Jesus, [the law of my new being], has freed me from the law of sin and death. [Therefore, every cancer cell and free radical that comes near my body dies instantly. Every terminal illness, sickness, and disease that comes near my body dies instantly, in the Name of Jesus. My immune system is protecting every part of my body. Every infection, plague, virus, bacteria, fungus, and germ that comes near my body, I demand dies instantly. Sickness and disease cannot live, bear fruit, or eat the fruit of my body, in the Name of Jesus. There are no mutant cells, free radicals, cancerous tumors, cysts, growths, masses, lesions, nodules, or lumps any where in my body. My marrow is making perfect blood and my blood is taking the life of God from my head to my toe. The law of the Spirit of life in Christ Jesus, is preserving all my vital organs: my heart, bones, joints, liver, kidneys, skin, in-testines, brain, eyes, colon, voice box, spine, limbs, pancreas, lungs, (*include any additional organs and parts of your anatomy*)

_____, _____, _____, _____,
_____, _____, _____, _____,
_____, _____, _____, _____,
_____, _____, _____, _____. God is honoring me and my entire household with long life and divine health], in the Name of Jesus.

HUMAN ANATOMY

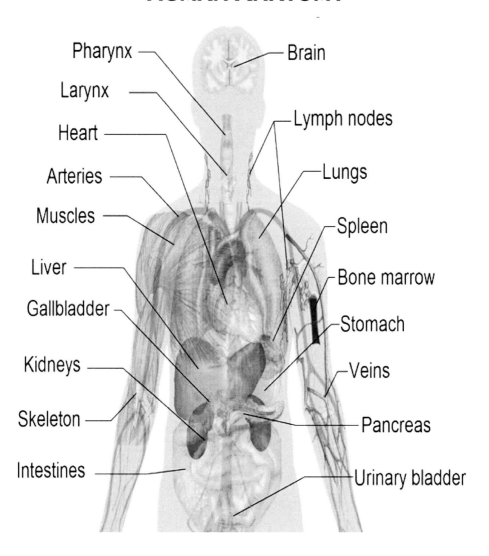

Pharynx — Brain

Larynx —

Lymph nodes

Heart —

Arteries —

Lungs

Muscles —

Spleen

Liver —

Bone marrow

Gallbladder —

Stomach

Kidneys —

Veins

Skeleton —

Pancreas

Intestines —

Urinary bladder

The life of God is flowing in every organ of my body, in the Name of Jesus.

Parts of the Human Brain

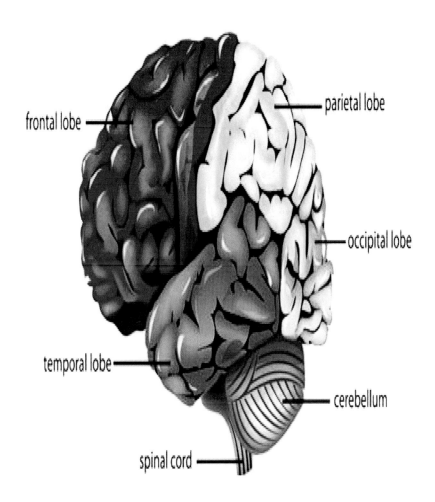

The life of God is flowing in every organ of my body, in the Name of Jesus.

HEART

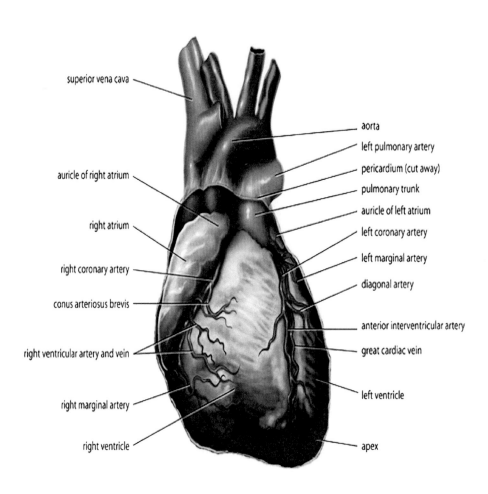

superior vena cava

aorta

left pulmonary artery

pericardium (cut away)

auricle of right atrium

pulmonary trunk

auricle of left atrium

right atrium

left coronary artery

left marginal artery

right coronary artery

diagonal artery

conus arteriosus brevis

anterior interventricular artery

great cardiac vein

right ventricular artery and vein

right marginal artery

left ventricle

right ventricle

apex

The life of God is flowing in every organ of my body, in the Name of Jesus.

KIDNEY

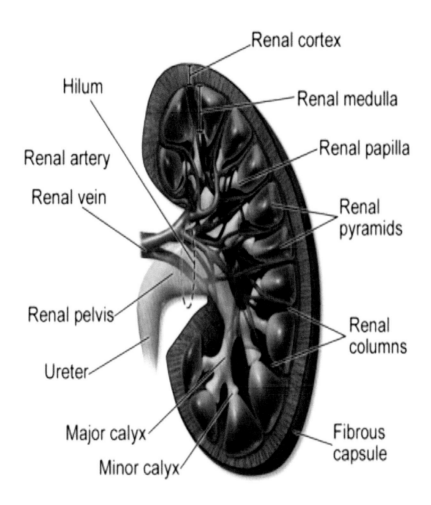

The life of God is flowing in every organ of my body, in the Name of Jesus.

My Longevity

CONFESSION

Proverbs 3:1-2 (AMP) Father, I will not forget Your law or Your teaching, but I let my heart keep Your commandments. Now my life is full of length of days, and years of a life [worth living], tranquility [inward, outward, and continuing through advanced, old age till death], are being added to me [and my best days and years of life are ahead of me], in the Name of Jesus.

Proverbs 4:10 (AMP) I am receiving Your sayings and the years of my life shall be many, in the Name of Jesus.

Psalm 91:16 (KJV) Father, thank You for satisfying me with long life and showing me Your salvation, in the Name of Jesus.

Isaiah 65:22 (AMP) Thank You Father, I am not building for another to inhabit and I am not planting for another to eat the [fruit] of my prosperity. For as the days of a tree, so shall my days be (here on earth), for I am one of Your chosen and elect. My life shall be long and I shall make use of and enjoy the works of my hands, in the Name of Jesus.

Job 5:26 (AMP) Glory to God, I shall come to my grave at a ripe OLD age and as a shock of grain goes up [to the threshing floor] in its season, in the Name of Jesus.

Psalm 103:5 (AMP) Father I praise You, for satisfying my mouth with good things, so that my youth is renewed like the eagles, in the Name of Jesus.

1 Thessalonians 5:23 (KJV) The God of all peace is sanctifying my whole spirit, soul, and body, preserving it blameless unto the coming of the Lord Jesus Christ, in the Name of Jesus.

Activating the Blessing of the Lord For Finances

CONFESSION

Genesis 1:26 (AMP) Father, You [Father, Son, and Holy Spirit] have made me in Your image and in Your likeness. You have given me complete authority over the fish of the sea, the birds of the air, the [tame] beasts, and over all of the earth, and over everything that creeps upon the earth. I receive Your plan and I act upon my authority now, in Jesus Name.

Proverbs 10:22 (AMP) Father, I activate the power of Your Blessing on my life. The Blessing is making me [truly] rich and adding no sorrow with it. My toil is not increasing it, for the Blessing is making me rich even while I am sleeping, in the Name of Jesus.

Genesis 12:2-3 (AMP) Father, I receive the power of Your Blessing on my life and my family. You are making us into a great nation, blessing us with abundant favors, making our names famous and distinguished. By Your Blessing, we are dispensing good to others. Thank You for blessing those who bless us, [who confer prosperity or happiness upon us] and cursing him who curses or uses insolent language toward us, for by us all the families and kindred of the earth are blessed {and by us they will bless themselves}, in the Name of Jesus.

By the Force of Righteousness, the Anointing, the Blessing of the Lord, and the Power of Grace through faith, I take dominion over the wealth and riches of the earth. I demand all riches and resources are coming in for myself and my family today, in the Name of Jesus.

Reaping My Harvest

Mark 10:29-30 (AMP)

[29] *Jesus said, Truly I tell you, there is no one who has given up and left house or brothers or sisters or mother or father or children or lands for My sake and for the Gospel's* [30] *Who will not receive a hundred times as much now in this time—houses and brothers and sisters and mothers and children and lands, with persecutions—and in the age to come eternal life.*

2 Corinthians 9:8, 10-11 (AMP)

[8] *And God is able to make all grace (every favor and earthly blessing) come to you in abundance, so that you may always and under all circumstances and whatever the need be self-sufficient [possessing enough to require no aid or support and furnished in abundance for every good work and charitable donation].* [10] *And [God] Who provides seed for the sower and bread for eating will also provide and multiply your [resources for] sowing and increase the fruits of your righteousness [which manifests itself in active goodness, kindness, and charity].* [11] *Thus you will be enriched in all things and in every way, so that you can be generous, and [your generosity as it is] administered by us will bring forth thanksgiving to God.*

Luke 6:38 (AMP)

[38] *Give, and [gifts] will be given to you; good measure, pressed down, shaken together, and running over, will they pour into [the pouch formed by] the bosom [of your robe and used as a bag]. For with the measure you deal out [with the measure you use when you confer benefits on others], it will be measured back to you.*

Reaping My Harvest

CONFESSION

Father, thank You for the hundred fold return on everything I have given up for Your sake and the sake of the Gospel. I receive a hundred times more in this life, right now, and in the age to come eternal life. I give You praise for making all grace (every favor and earthly blessing) come to me in abundance. Now I always, under all circumstances and whatever the need, am self-sufficient possessing enough, and requiring no aid or support. You have given me seed to sow and have multiplied my resources for sowing and have increased in me all righteousness. Now I can and do give generously to bring forth thanksgiving to You, in the Name of Jesus.

I am giving gifts generously and now gifts are being given to me in good measure, pressed down, shaken together, and running over. People are pouring gifts into my bosom, in the Name of Jesus. By the power of the Anointing and the Blessing of the Lord, I take dominion over the wealth and riches of the earth and I demand all these riches and resources are coming in for myself and my family daily, in the Name of Jesus.

Make a list of the riches that God has given you.

Father, in the Name of Jesus, I believe we have received...

_____

_____

_____

_____

_____

Make a list of the riches that God has given you.

Father, in the Name of Jesus, I believe we have received...

_____

_____

_____

_____

_____

_____

_____

_____

_____

_____

_____

_____

_____

_____

_____

_____

Make a list of the riches that God has given you.

Father, in the Name of Jesus, I believe we have received...

_____

_____

_____

_____

_____

_____

_____

_____

_____

_____

_____

_____

_____

_____

_____

Success of My Plans & Goals

Proverbs 16:3 (AMP)
³ *Roll your works upon the Lord [commit and trust them wholly to Him]; He will cause your thoughts to become agreeable to His will, And so shall your plans be established and succeed.*

CONFESSION

Father, I am rolling all my works and plans on You. Thank You for causing all my thoughts to become agreeable to Your will, so all my plans are established and succeeding, in the Name of Jesus.

Abundant results are coming forth in my life today unto the glory of God. EVERTYHING I'm doing is thriving, flourishing, and multiplying rapidly. I'm taking in the mega harvest of the earth in all good things, in the Name of Jesus.

Mathew 25:2,4 (AMP) In the Name of Jesus, I am like the five wise virgins in all the works of my hands. I master over time and I am never late, because I am sensible, intelligent, and prudent in every area of my life.

My Plans and Goals

January Plans Established

1. _____

2. _____

3. _____

4. _____

5. _____

February Plans Established

1. _____

2. _____

3. _____

4. _____

5. _____

March Plans Established

1. _____

2. _____

3. _____

4. _____

5. _____

April Plans Established

1. _____

2. _____

3. _____

4. _____

5. _____

May Plans Established

1. _____

2. _____

3. _____

4. _____

5. _____

June Plans Established

1. _____

2. _____

3. _____

4. _____

5. _____

July Plans Established

1. _____

2. _____

3. _____

4. _____

5. _____

August Plans Established

1. _____

2. _____

3. _____

4. _____

5. _____

September Plans Established

1. _____

2. _____

3. _____

4. _____

5. _____

October Plans Established

1. _____
2. _____
3. _____
4. _____
5. _____

November Plans Established

1. _____
2. _____
3. _____
4. _____
5. _____

December Plans Established

1. _____
2. _____
3. _____
4. _____
5. _____

Seedtime & Harvest

Revelation 14:15 (MSG)

[15] *Another Angel came out of the Temple, shouting to the Cloud-Enthroned, "Swing your sickle and reap. It's harvest time. Earth's harvest is ripe for reaping."*

Mark 4:26-32 (KJV)

[26] *And He said, The kingdom of God is like a man who scatters seed upon the ground,*

[27] *And then continues sleeping and rising night and day while the seed sprouts and grows and increases—he knows not how.*

[28] *The earth produces [acting] by itself—first the blade, then the ear, then the full grain in the ear.*

[29] *But when the grain is ripe and permits, immediately he sends forth [the reapers] and puts in the sickle, because the harvest stands ready.*

[30] *And He said, With what can we compare the kingdom of God, or what parable shall we use to illustrate and explain it?*

[31] *It is like a grain of mustard seed, which, when sown upon the ground, is the smallest of all seeds upon the earth;*

[32] *Yet after it is sown, it grows up and becomes the greatest of all garden herbs and puts out large branches, so that the birds of the air are able to make nests and dwell in its shade.*

Father, I receive my mega harvest, in the Name of Jesus.

Date	Seed	Harvest
_____	_____	_____
_____	_____	_____
_____	_____	_____
_____	_____	_____

Seedtime & Harvest

Date	Seed	Harvest
_____	_____	_____
_____	_____	_____
_____	_____	_____
_____	_____	_____
_____	_____	_____
_____	_____	_____
_____	_____	_____
_____	_____	_____
_____	_____	_____
_____	_____	_____
_____	_____	_____
_____	_____	_____
_____	_____	_____
_____	_____	_____
_____	_____	_____
_____	_____	_____
_____	_____	_____
_____	_____	_____

Seedtime & Harvest

Date	Seed	Harvest
____	_____	_____
____	_____	_____
____	_____	_____
____	_____	_____
____	_____	_____
____	_____	_____
____	_____	_____
____	_____	_____
____	_____	_____
____	_____	_____
____	_____	_____
____	_____	_____
____	_____	_____
____	_____	_____
____	_____	_____
____	_____	_____
____	_____	_____
____	_____	_____
____	_____	_____

Romans 8:26-28 (AMP)

[26] So too the [Holy] Spirit comes to our aid and bears us up in our weakness; for we do not know what prayer to offer nor how to offer it worthily as we ought, but the Spirit Himself goes to meet our supplication and pleads in our behalf with unspeakable yearnings and groanings too deep for utterance. [27] And He Who searches the hearts of men knows what is in the mind of the [Holy] Spirit [what His intent is], because the Spirit intercedes and pleads [before God] in behalf of the saints according to and in harmony with God's will. [28] We are assured and know that [God being a partner in their labor] all things work together and are [fitting into a plan] for good to and for those who love God and are called according to [His] design and purpose.

Jude 1:20 (AMP)

[20] But you, beloved, build yourselves up [founded] on your most holy faith [make progress, rise like an edifice higher and higher], praying in the Holy Spirit;

CONFESSION

Father, as I prepare to leave and start my day, I pray in the Holy Spirit (in other tongues) releasing all the mysteries of the divine appointments, opportunities, and Your abilities that are awaiting me.

Ready, Set & Go

Father, I thank You for what You have prepared for me and I am sensitive and responsive to all of the leadings of the Holy Spirit. I am not shrinking back in fear or overriding the supernatural leadings of the Holy Spirit. Today, Your power is being demonstrated through me, in the Name of Jesus.

Holy Spirit, I yield my tongue, my spirit, soul, and my body to You. Take complete control of my life that I may be glorified and glorify my Father God, in the Powerful Name of Jesus.

Now that you have prayed out the mysteries awaiting you in other tongues, go forth and have a wonderful day!

Job 32:8 (NLT)

But there is a spirit within people, the breath of the Almighty within them, that makes them intelligent.

Meditation:

The breath of the Almighty is within my spirit, making me intelligent [eloquent, prudent, skilled, wise, diligent, and full of understanding and discernment], separating and distinguishing me mentally, in the Name of Jesus.

The Word Of God Is A Lamp Unto My Feet And A Light Unto My Path, in the Name of Jesus.

Personalized Prayers
For
Every Area

PERSONALIZED PRAYERS FOR EVERY AREA

We have included personalized prayers, written in first person, present-tense for you, that cover numerous topics. The Bible says, *"all the Promises of God in Him are yes and in Him Amen, unto the glory of God by us" (2 Cor.1:20 KJV)*. God has loaded our lives with tons of benefits, but faith is required to experience them all. Reading the Promises of God in present-tense, helps you to feed and activate your faith, while creating the right visions and imaginations of yourself and your life.

God has created a perfect plan for your life and family *(Jer. 29:11 KJV)* and His Word is full of power to bring it to pass, when mixed with faith. Reading the Promises of God on a regular basis in first person present-tense, keeps building your faith for an extraordinary life from one degree to the next. You will find yourself growing in the ability to trust God in all things and receive His grace through faith, to handle whatever needs may arise.

Never forget that in order for His Word to come to pass in your life, you MUST receive it by faith. May your faith stay strong as you allow God to move through your faith to create His glorious plan.

Pastor Sandy

☎ AUTHORITY IN THE NAME OF JESUS

Matthew 28:18 (AMP) Praise God, Jesus said, "All authority (all power of rule) in heaven and on earth has been given to Me." I believe it and I receive all the authority and power of rule that is in the Name of Jesus. Now, I am ruling in the earth because all the power of the heavens and earth are accommodating me and obeying my commands, in the Name of Jesus.

Colossians 2:10 (AMP) Thank You Father, for putting me in Christ, making me full and bringing me to the fullness of life [in Christ I am filled with the Godhead—Father, Son and Holy Spirit— and I am reaching full spiritual stature]. And He is the Head of all rule and authority [of every angelic principality and power]. Now, in the Name of Jesus I rule and exercise authority over every angelic principality and power.

Mark 16:17-18, 20 (AMP) I am preaching and publishing the Gospel to the whole world, just as Jesus commanded. These attesting signs accompany me because I believe in the Name of Jesus: I drive out demons; I speak in new languages, I pick up serpents; and [even] if I drink anything deadly, it will not hurt me; I lay my hands on the sick, and they get well. As I go out and preach everywhere, the Lord keeps working with me and confirming the message by the attesting signs *and* miracles that closely accompany me [it]. Amen (so be it), in the Name of Jesus.

John 14:12-14 (AMP) Praise the Lord! Just as Jesus said, because I am steadfastly believing on the Lord Jesus Christ, I am enabled to do the things that He did and even greater things. The Lord Himself is granting whatever I ask in His Name [as I present all that He is and all that He has done] and now the Father is glorified and extolled in (through) the Son. Just as the Lord promised,

He is granting [He Himself is doing for me] whatever I ask in the Name of Jesus [as I present all that He is and has done].

Philippians 2:9-11 (AMP) Glory to God! The Lord Jesus stooped so low and God has highly exalted Him and has freely bestowed on Him the name that is above every name. Now in (at) the Name of Jesus every knee should (must) bow, in heaven and on earth and under the earth. And every tongue [frankly and openly] confess *and* acknowledge that Jesus Christ is Lord, all to the glory of God the Father.

Proverbs 18:10 (AMP) The Name of the Lord is the strong tower for my family and I; we are the [consistently] righteous [upright and in right standing with God]. We have run into it and we are safe, high [above evil] *and* strong, in the Name of Jesus.

☎ CONFIDENCE IN THE LORD

Numbers 23:19-20 (AMP) My God is not a man, that He should tell or act a lie, neither the son of man that He should feel repentance or compunction [for what He has promised me]. He never says it to not do it. Nor has He spoken (His Promise) to not make it good in my life. God has commanded His blessing upon me and what He has blessed, no one can reverse or qualify it, in the Name of Jesus.

Isaiah 55:10-11 (AMP) Just as the rain and snow come down from the heavens, and return not there again, but waters the earth and makes it bring forth and sprout, that it may give seed to the sower and bread to the eater, Your Word is not void [without producing any effect, useless], in my life. Father, I praise You because Your Word is accomplishing what You please and purposed. It is prospering in me and for me, just as You sent it, in the Name of Jesus.

Deuteronomy 7:9 (AMP) Father, I know, recognize, and understand that You are God, the faithful God, Who is keeping Your covenant. Your steadfast love and mercy is with us, because we love You and we are keeping Your commandments. You are keeping your covenant with me and my family to a thousand generations, in the Name of Jesus.

2 Corinthians 6:18 (KJV) Father, I receive Your promise to me, "And I will be a Father to you, and you shall be My sons and daughters, says the Lord Almighty." I take all the love, care, faithfulness, protection and all the goodness that comes from You being my Father and I thank You for it, in the Name of Jesus.

1 Kings 8:56 (KJV) I bless You Lord, for You have given us according to all that You Promised. Not one Word has failed of all Your good Promises, which You promised us, in the Name of Jesus.

1 Corinthians 1:9 (AMP) Thank You Father, for being faithful reliable, trustworthy, and therefore ever true to Your promises to me and I am depending on every Word. By You I have been called into companionship and participation with Your Son, Jesus Christ my Lord, in the Name of Jesus.

Hebrews 6:17-18 (AMP) Accordingly Father, in Your desire to show more convincingly and beyond doubt to us, who have inherited Your promise; the unchangeableness of Your purpose and plan for us, has intervened (mediated) with an oath. By two unchangeable things [Your promise and Your oath] it is impossible for You ever to prove false or deceive us. We have fled [to You} for our refuge and now we have a mighty indwelling strength and strong encouragement to grasp and hold fast to the hope appointed for us and set before us, in the Name of Jesus.

Luke 1:37 *(AMP)* Glory to God, the impossible has become possible for me. With my God nothing is ever impossible and no Word from God is without power or impossible of fulfillment, in the Name of Jesus.

☎DEBT FREEDOM

Romans 13:8 (AMP) Father, according to your command, I am keeping out of debt and You are prospering my life, so now I owe no man anything except love. By practicing love to others I am fulfilling the Law, in the Name Jesus.

Deuteronomy 28:43-44 (KJV) Father, You have given me the Blessing to live free from debt and bondage. I decree by the power of the Blessing that no foreigners living around me will become stronger and stronger than I and I will not become weaker and weaker. I do not have to borrow money from them, but I am empowered to lend money to them. By the power of the Blessing I am the head and they are the tail, in the Name of Jesus.

Deuteronomy 15:5-6 (AMP) I am only listening to the voice of the Lord my God, to do watchfully all the commandments that He is giving me today. The Lord is blessing me as He promised and now I am lending to many nations and ruling over many nations and they are not ruling over me, in the Name of Jesus.

1 John 5:4-5 (AMP) I am born of God and I am victorious over the world and it's system of debt. I have overcome it and conquered debt by my faith, because I believe that Jesus is the Son of God and I am adhering to, trusting in and relying on that fact. I see myself as debt free and every decision I make is in respect to that freedom, in the Name of Jesus.

Psalm 85:8-9 (AMP) I am listening [with expectancy] to what God the Lord will say and is saying to me. For He is speaking peace to me and to His saints (those who are in right standing with Him); I am not turning again to [self-confident] folly [debt]. Surely God's salvation is near to me and all who reverently *and* worshipfully fear Him, [those ready to appropriate it] and now the manifestation of the presence of God, His glory is like a tabernacle abiding in my land, in the Name of Jesus.

☎ MY DESTINY

Acts 17:26-28 (AMP) Praise God, You have made me from one [common origin, one source, one blood] of all nations of men to settle on the face of the earth. You have definitely determined [my] allotted period of time and the fixed boundaries of my habitation, my settlements, lands, and abodes, so as I am seeking You, I am finding You, for You are not far from me. For in You I live and move and have my being; just as some of Your [own] poets have said, I am also Your offspring, in the Name of Jesus.

Psalm 31:15-16 (AMP) Father, I am thankful that my times are in Your hands; and that You have delivered me from the hands of my foes [from those who pursue me and persecute me]. Your face Is shining on me and I am saved for Your mercy's sake and in Your loving-kindness, in the Name of Jesus.

Psalm 31:19-20 (AMP) Oh, how great is Your goodness, which You have laid up for me, because I fear, revere, and worship You. I see the goodness which You have wrought for me, because I am trusting and taking refuge in You before the sons of men! In the secret place of Your presence, You are hiding me from the plots of men and You are keeping me secretly in Your pavilion from the strife of tongues, in the Name of Jesus.

Joshua 24:15-16 (KJV) It may seem evil to the world to serve the Lord, but as for me and my house, we will serve the Lord, for we say, "Far be it from us to forsake the Lord to serve other gods," in the Name of Jesus.

☎ DELIVERANCE FROM SIN

Roman 6:14 (AMP) I declare that sin no longer exerts dominion over me, since I am not under the Law as a slave, but under grace, a subject of God's favor and mercy, in the Name of Jesus.

1 Corinthians 9:27 (KJV) I discipline my body and make it my slave; training it to do what it should do and not what it shouldn't. I don't allow overeating, bondage, lust, or sin of any kind in my body. I will not be disqualified after I preach the Gospel, in the Name of Jesus.

☎ DIVINE GUIDANCE

Colossians 3:15 (AMP) My family and I let the peace (soul harmony which comes) from Christ rule (act as umpire continually) in our hearts, [deciding and settling with finality all questions that arise in our minds, in this peaceful state] to which as [members of Christ's] one body we also live as we are called. We are thankful and appreciative, giving praise to You Father, in the Name of Jesus.

James 1:5 (AMP) Father, I ask for Your divine wisdom for every aspect of my life today. You are the giving God Who gives it to me liberally and ungrudgingly, without reproaching or faultfinding. Now I receive it by faith without wavering and I say, "I know what to do in every situation today, for I have divine wisdom from my Father God, in the Name of Jesus."

☎DIVINE PROTECTION

Proverbs 2:7-8 (AMP) Thank You Father, for hiding away sound and godly Wisdom, and storing it for me (because I am upright and in right standing with You). You are a shield to me because I walk uprightly and in integrity so You can guard my paths in justice. Yes, You are preserving me as one of Your saints, in the Name of Jesus.

Proverbs 4:5-6 (AMP) Glory to God, I am getting skillful and godly Wisdom, and understanding (discernment, comprehension, and interpretation). I am not forgetting and I do not turn back from the words of your mouth. I am not forsaking [Wisdom], and she is keeping, defending and protecting me. I love her and she is guarding me, in the Name of Jesus.

John 17:15 (AMP) Father, I receive the prayer that Jesus prayed for me. Thank You for not taking me out of the world, but You are keeping and protecting me and my family from the evil one, in the Name of Jesus.

Psalm 121:2-8 (AMP) Father, I thank You for being my help, You, Who made heaven and earth. For You are not allowing my foot to slip or to be moved and You, Who keeps me will not slumber. You are my keeper, and my shade on my right hand [the side not carrying a shield]. The sun shall not smite me by day, nor the moon by night. For You, Lord are keeping me from all evil; You are keeping my life. You are keeping my going out and my coming in from this time forth and forevermore, in the Name of Jesus.

Psalm 4:8 (KJV) Father, I thank You that in peace I will both lie down and sleep, for You, Lord alone make me and my household dwell in safety and we are confidently trusting in You, in the Name of Jesus.

Psalm 3:5 (AMP) Glory to God, every night I lay down, sleep and I wake again, for the Lord is sustaining me, in the Name of Jesus.

☎ <u>MY DOMINION</u>

Ephesians 5:1 (AMP) Father, I am imitating You [copying You and following Your example], as a well-beloved child [imitates his father], in the Name of Jesus.

1 Peter 2:21 (AMP) Father, I glorify You for sending Christ to suffer for me, leaving me an example, so now I am following in His footsteps. I know that I was called to this [it is inseparable from my vocation], in the Name of Jesus.

Psalm 8:6 (KJV) Thank You Father, for making me have dominion over the works of Your Hands and putting all things under my feet, in the Name of Jesus.

Genesis 27:28-29 (AMP) Father, I praise You for giving me and my household the dew of the heavens and of the fatness of the earth and abundance of grain and [new] wine. Thank You, for causing people to serve us and nations to bow down to us. You are making us masters in the earth. Everyone who curses us is cursed and favor with blessings is on those who bless us, in the Name of Jesus.

Genesis 1:26 (KJV) Father, just as You said, You have made me in Your image, after Your likeness. Now I have complete authority over the fish of the sea, the birds of the air, the [tame] beasts, over all of the earth, and over everything that creeps upon the earth, in the Name of Jesus.

Leviticus 26:4-6 (AMP) Thank You Father, for giving me rain in due season, so my land is yielding her increase and the trees of the field are yielding their fruit. My threshing [time] is reaching to the vintage and the vintage [time] is reaching to the sowing time, and I am eating my bread to the full and I am dwelling in my land securely. I praise You for giving me peace in the land; so now when I lie down, no one can fill me with dread or make me afraid. For You have cleared the ferocious (wild) beasts out of my land, and there is no sword going through my land, in the Name of Jesus.

☎ DOUBLE FOLD RESTORATION HARVEST

Isaiah 61:7 (AMP) Praise God! Instead of my former shame I have a two-fold recompense. Instead of dishonor and reproach I am rejoicing in my portion. In my land I am possessing double what I had forfeited and everlasting joy is mine, in the Name of Jesus.

Zechariah 9:12 (AMP) I have returned to the Lord (the stronghold of my security and prosperity). Father, I believe I receive double restoration of my former prosperity today, according to Your promise, in the Name of Jesus.

Psalm 126:1 (AMP) Father, You have done great things for us! Thank You for turning to freedom our captivity and restoring our fortunes. Though we sowed in tears, we are reaping in joy and singing, in the Name of Jesus.

☎ FAVOR OF GOD

Proverbs 3:3-4 (KJV) My family and I do not let mercy and truth forsake us; we have bound them about our necks and written them upon the tables of our heart. For we find favor and a good understanding in the sight of God and man in every situation, in the Name of Jesus.

Esther 2:15 (AMP) I find favor and kindness in the eyes of all who see me, now rules and regulations are reversed, policies are broken and exceptions are made for me, and I receive preferential treatment wherever I go, in the Name of Jesus.

Ecclesiastes 10:12 (AMP) The words of my mouth are gracious and win me favor, like those of the wise man's, in the Name of Jesus.

Luke 3:52 (AMP) Glory to God, I am increasing in wisdom (in broad and full understanding) and in stature and years, and in favor with God and man, in the Name of Jesus.

Psalm 5:12 (AMP) I praise and glorify You Father, for blessing me, because I am one of the [uncompromisingly] righteous [I am upright and in right standing with You]; Thank You for surrounding me with goodwill (pleasure and favor) as with a shield, in the Name of Jesus.

☎ FORGIVENESS

Mark 11:25 (AMP) Father, as I stand before You, I forgive those who have hurt me and done wrong to me. I forgive them and I let it drop (leaving it and letting it go) in order that You Father, Who is in heaven may also forgive me of my [own] failings and shortcomings and let them drop, in the Name of Jesus.

Luke 23:34 (KJV) Father, I pray and ask You to forgive my enemies, for they know not what they do, in the Name of Jesus?

☎ FORGETTING THE PAST

Isaiah 43:18-19 (KJV) I thank You Lord, that I do not remember the things that happened before and I do not think about the past. You are doing a new thing and it is happening now. You are making roads for me in the wilderness and rivers in the desert, in the Name of Jesus.

Philippians 3:13-14 (KJV) I forget everything that is behind me and I lengthen my stride, running towards that which is ahead of me, in the Name of Jesus.

☎ FREEDOM FROM FEAR

2 Timothy 1:7(AMP) God has not given me a spirit of timidity, of cowardice, of craven, and cringing, and fawning fear but [He has given me a spirit] of power, and of love, and of calm, and well-balanced mind with discipline and self-control, in the Name of Jesus.

Isaiah 41:10 (AMP) I will not fear, for there is nothing to fear, for the Lord my God is with me. I will not look around in terror and be dismayed, for God is my God and He is strengthening me, hardening me to difficulties, helping me, holding me up, and retaining me with His victorious right hand of rightness and justice, in the Name of Jesus.

☎ HUMILITY

James 4:10 (AMP) Father, I am humbling myself [I feel very insignificant] in Your presence and now You are exalting me [You are lifting me up and making my life significant], in the Name of Jesus.

Job 22:23 (AMP) Father, I have returned to You, the Almighty [I submit and humble myself before You], now I am being built up because I have put away unrighteousness far from my tent, in the Name of Jesus.

☎ HEALTH & BEAUTY

Deuteronomy 7:13-15 (MSG) Thank You Father, for loving me, blessing me, and increasing me. You are blessing the babies from my womb and the harvest of grain, new wine, and the oil from my fields. You are blessing the calves from my herds and lambs from my flocks in the country, You promised my ancestors that you'd give me. I glorify You for blessing me beyond all other peoples; there's no sterility or barrenness in me or my animals. Father, You have gotten rid of all sickness and all the evil afflictions experienced in Egypt [the world], and You have put not one on me, but on those who hate me, in the Name of Jesus.

1 Kings 8:56 (MSG) Blessed be my Father God, who has given peace to me and my family, just as He said He'd do. Not one of all the good and wonderful words that He has spoke to us has misfired, in the Name of Jesus.

Psalm 103:1-5 (MSG) O my soul, bless GOD. From my head to my toe, I bless His holy name! O my soul, bless God, I will not forget a single blessing! Thank You Father, for forgiving my sins, every one. Healing my diseases, every one. You have redeem me from hell, and saved my life! You have crowned me with love and mercy, a paradise crown. I praise You for wrapping me in goodness, and beauty eternal. You have renewed my youth, for I am always young in Your presence, in the Name of Jesus.

Psalm 118:17 (AMP) Father, I praise You for giving me a long life. I shall not die but live, and I will declare the works *and* recount the illustrious acts that You have done, in the Name of Jesus.

Exodus 23:25-26 (AMP) Glory to God, I am serving the Lord my God and He is blessing my bread and water, and taking sickness from my midst. Just as You have promised, none in my family shall lose their young by miscarriage or be barren in our land, and You are fulfilling the number of my days, in the Name of Jesus.

Proverbs 4:20-23 (AMP) I am attending to Your words Father, consenting and submitting to Your sayings. I am not letting them depart from my sight and keeping them in the center of my heart.

For they are life to me, healing and health to all my flesh. I am keeping and guarding my heart with all vigilance and above all that I guard, for out of it is flowing the springs of life, in the Name of Jesus.

John 10:10 (AMP) The Lord came so that I may have and enjoy my life, and have it in abundance (to the full, till it overflows), and I receive it, in the Name of Jesus.

Jeremiah 1:12 (AMP) Thank You Father for healing me! For I see well that You are alert and active, watching over Your Word to perform it in my body, in the Name of Jesus.

1 Peter 2:24 (AMP) Thank You Lord, for personally bearing my sins in Your [own] body on the tree [as on an alter and offering Yourself on it], that I might die (cease to exist) to sin and live to righteousness. I boldly declare that by Your wounds, I have been healed, in the Name of Jesus.

Genesis 12:11 (AMP) Father, I praise You, for You have made me beautiful to behold, and all that look upon me know it, in the Name of Jesus.

1 Samuel 16:12 (AMP) Let all the praise and glory be unto You Father! I have a healthy complexion and beautiful eyes, and I am fine-looking. Thank You for choosing and anointing me, in the Name of Jesus.

1 Samuel 25:3 (AMP) Father, I thank You for giving me good understanding and making me beautiful, in the Name of Jesus.

2 Samuel 14:25 (AMP) Unto the glory of God, I say that in all the earth, I am praised for my beauty; from the sole of my foot to the crown of my head there is no blemish on me, in the Name of Jesus.

Esther 1:11 (AMP) I praise You Father, for bringing me before kings, princes and peoples to show them my beauty, for You have made me fair to look at, in the Name of Jesus.

Matthew 10:30 (AMP) Praise the Lord, all the hairs on my head are numbered and are maintained at the original count [I am not losing any], in the Name of Jesus.

Luke 21:18 (AMP) Glory to God, not a hair on my head shall perish. [All of my hair is thriving, multiplying, and flourishing], in the Name of Jesus.

Ezekiel 16:7 (AMP) Father, You are causing me to multiply as the bud which grows in the field, and causing me to increase and become tall and full of maidenhood and beauty; my breasts formed and my hair grown, in the Name of Jesus.

☎ OPERATING IN THE LOVE OF GOD

Ezekiel 36:26-27 (BBE) I praise You Father, for giving me a new heart and putting a new spirit within me. Thank You for taking away the heart of stone from my flesh and giving me a heart of flesh. You have put Your Spirit in me and now I am guided by Your rules, keeping Your orders and doing them, in the Name of Jesus.

1 Corinthians 13:4-8 (AMP) Glory to God, My love is enduring long, for I am patient and kind; I am never envious nor do I boil over with jealousy; I am not boastful or vainglorious, and I do not display myself haughtily. I am not conceited (arrogant and inflated with pride); I am never rude (unmannerly), and I do not act unbecomingly. My love [God's love in me] does not insist on its own rights or its own way, for I am not self-seeking; touchy or fretful or resentful; and I take no account of the evil done to me, nor do I pay attention to a suffered wrong. I never rejoice at injustice and unrighteousness, but I rejoice when right and truth prevail. My love is bearing up under anything and everything that comes and I am ever ready to believe the best of every person, my hopes are fadeless under all circumstances, and endures everything [without weakening]. My love never fails, in the Name of Jesus.

Ephesians 3:16-19 (AMP) Father, I thank You for granting unto me, out of the rich treasury of Your glory, to be strengthened and reinforced with mighty power in my inner man by the Holy Spirit [Himself indwelling my innermost being and personality]. Christ, through my faith is [actually] dwelling (settled down, abiding, made His permanent home) in my heart! I am rooted deep in love and founded securely on love. I have the power and I am strong to apprehend and grasp with all the saints [God's devoted people, the experience of that love], what is the breadth and length and height and depth of it. I am coming to know [practically, through experience for myself] the love of Christ, which far surpasses mere knowledge [without experience]. I am filled through all my being unto the fullness of You [having the richest measure of Your divine presence], and I am becoming a body wholly filled and flooded with You Father (God Himself), in the Name of Jesus.

☎ MEDITATING THE WORD OF GOD

Joshua 1:8 (AMP) This Book of the Law is not departing out of my of my mouth, but I am meditating on it day and night, observing and doing according to all that is written in it. Now, I am making my way prosperous and dealing wisely, and having good success, in the Name of Jesus.

Psalm 1:1-3 (KJV) Praise God! I am blessed because I do not walk in the counsel of the ungodly, nor standeth in the way of sinners, nor sitteth in the seat of the scornful. I delight in the Law of the Lord, and meditate in His law day and night. Now my life is like a tree planted by the rives of water, that bringeth forth fruit in it's season. My leaf also does not wither, and whatsoever I do prospers, in the Name of Jesus.

☎ GRACE OF GOD

Acts 4:33 (AMP) In the Name of Jesus, I am full of great strength, ability, *and* power, delivering my testimony to the resurrection of the Lord Jesus, and great grace (loving-kindness, favor and good-will) is resting richly upon me.

Matthew 11:28-30 (MSG) Glory to God! I am no longer tired, worn out and burned out on religion. I am keeping company with the grace of God. Daily I am getting away with His grace and recovering my life. Grace is teaching me how to take a real rest. I am talking and working with grace, watching how grace does it. I am learning the unforced rhythms of grace, Who is not laying anything heavy or ill-fitting on me. Now I am living my life freely and lightly, in the Name of Jesus.

Ephesians 2:8 (AMP) Father, I praise You for Your free grace (Your unmerited favor) that is saving me (delivering me from judgment *and* making me a partaker of Christ's salvation) through [my] faith. And this [salvation] is not of myself [of my own doing, it came not through my own striving], but it is Your Gift to me, in the Name of Jesus.

☎ MARRIAGE & FAMILY
MARRIAGE
Psalm 5:12 (KJV) Thank You Father, for surrounding me with favor as with a shield [therefore I have favor in my spouse's eyes above every other man or woman on earth], in the Name of Jesus.

Proverbs 18:22 (AMP) God has led me to my true spouse and given me His favor in their eyes, in the Name of Jesus.

HUSBANDS

1 Peter 3:7 (AMP) Glory to God, I am a godly man after God's own heart. I live considerately with [my wife], and I have an intelligent recognition of our marriage relationship. I honor my wife as physically the weaker, but I realize that we are joint heirs of the grace {God's unmerited favor} of life, in order that my prayers may not be hindered and cut off. By this I am able to always pray effectively, in the Name of Jesus.

Genesis 2:24 (AMP) Praise God, I have left my father and mother, to become united with my wife and I am cleaving to her. We have become one flesh, in the Name of Jesus.

Ecclesiastes 9:9 (NLT) Father, I am living happily with the wife whom I will love all the days of my life, which You have given me under the sun. She is the reward that You have given me, for all my earthy toil, in the Name of Jesus.

Ephesians 5:25-26 (MSG) I am going all the way in love for my wife, exactly as Christ did for the Church. My love is marked by giving and not by getting. Just as Christ's love makes the Church whole, my love for my wife is making her whole. My words evoke her beauty and everything I do and say to her are designed to bring the best out of her, in the Name of Jesus.

Genesis 2:23 (AMP) Father, just as Adam said, I also say of my wife, "This [creature] is now bone of my bones and flesh of my flesh; she shall be called Woman, because she was taken out of a man," in the Name of Jesus.

2 Timothy 2:21 (AMP) Father, I cleanse myself from what is ignoble and unclean, and I separate myself from contact with contaminating and corrupting influences. Now, I am a vessel set apart and useful for honorable, and noble purposes, consecrated and profitable to You Master, fit, and ready for any good work [there is no perversion or immorality anywhere in my life], in the Name of Jesus.

WIVES

Song of Solomon 4:10-11 (AMP) Praise God, my husband continually says to me, "How beautiful is your love, my sister, my [promised] bride! How much better is your love than wine! And the fragrance of your ointments than all spices! Your lips, O my [promised] bride, drop honey as the honeycomb; and honey and milk are under your tongue. And the odor of your garments is like the odor of Lebanon," in the Name of Jesus.

Song of Solomon 4:7 (AMP) Glory to God, daily my husband exclaims to me, "O my love, how beautiful you are! There is no flaw in you," in the Name of Jesus.

Proverbs 5:15-20 (AMP) Father, I thank You that my husband drinks waters out of his own cistern [of a pure marriage relation-ship with me], and fresh running waters out of his own well. His offspring will not be dispersed abroad as water brooks in the streets. Praise God, my husband confines himself to me, [his own wife] letting his children be for him alone, and not the children of strangers with him. He is letting his fountain [of human life] be blessed [with the rewards of fidelity], and rejoicing with me, the wife of his youth. To my husband, I am as the loving hind and pleasant doe [tender, gentle, attractive]. He lets my bosom satisfy him at all times, and he is always transported with delight in my love, in the Name of Jesus.

Proverbs 12:4 (AMP) I declare by faith, that I am a virtuous and worthy wife [earnest and strong in character]. I am a crowning joy to my husband, in the Name of Jesus.

1 Peter 3:2-4 (AMP) Praise God, under all circumstances, my husband observes the pure and modest way in which I conduct myself, together with my reverence for him. I feel for him all that reverence includes: I respect, defer to, revere, honor, esteem appreciate, prize, and in the human sense, I adore him. I admire, praise, am devoted, deeply love, and enjoy my husband. My adorning is the incorruptible and unfading charm of a gentle and peaceful spirit, not [merely] eternal adorning with [elaborate] interweaving and knotting of my hair, the wearing of jewelry, or changes of clothes. I'm letting my beauty be the inward adorning and beauty of the hidden person of the heart. My beauty is that of a peaceful spirit, which [is not anxious or wrought up, but] is very precious in the sight of God, in the Name of Jesus.

Ephesians 5:25-26 (KJV) Father, I thank You for giving me a husband that loves me as Christ loved the Church and gave Himself up for her. So that He might sanctify her, having cleansed her by the washing of the water with the Word, in the Name of Jesus.

2 Timothy 2:21 (AMP) Father, I thank You for giving me a husband who has cleansed himself from what is ignoble and unclean and who separates himself from contact with contaminating and corrupting influences], in the Name of Jesus. My husband is a vessel set apart and useful for honorable and noble purposes, consecrated and profitable to the Master, fit and ready for any good work and I praise You for such an awesome husband, in the Name of Jesus.

Song of Solomon 4:9 (MSG) Thank You Father, for causing my husband to tell me daily, "You've captured my heart, dear friend. You looked at me, and I fell in love. One look my way and I was hopelessly in love!," in the Name of Jesus. Praise God!

Proverbs 19:13-14 (AMP) In the Name of Jesus, I am not a contentions wife, that is like a continual dripping [of water through a chink in the roof]. My husband has received houses and riches as an inheritance from his fathers, but I am a wise, understanding, *and* prudent wife, to my husband from the Lord.

CHILDREN

Proverbs 22:6 (AMP) Father, I am training up my children in the way they should go [and in keeping with their individual gift or bent], and when they are old they will not depart from it, in the Name of Jesus.

Deuteronomy 31:13 (AMP) Praise God, my children who have not known it, now hear and learn [reverently] to fear the Lord my God, as long as they live in the land which they have gone to possess, in the Name of Jesus.

Ephesians 6:1-3 (AMP) Thank God, my children obey their parents, for this is right. They honor (esteem and value as precious) their father and mother—parents in the Lord [as His representatives], for this is just and this is the first commandment with a promise—that all may be well with them and they will live long on the earth, in the Name of Jesus.

Isaiah 65:23 (AMP) In the Name of Jesus, all our labors are not in vain. We are not bringing forth our [children] for sudden terror or calamity; for they are our descendants, the blessed of the Lord, and their offspring shall also be with them, in the Name of Jesus.

☎ MY MIND

I Corinthians 2:16 (AMP) I have the mind of Christ, the Messiah, and I am holding the thoughts (feelings and purposes) of His heart. Therefore, I cast down every contrary and negative thought and I give You mastery over my mind Father, in the Name of Jesus.

James 1:5-6 (AMP) Father, I ask for Your wisdom for today and I receive it from You, right now by faith, without wavering, hesitating, or doubting. You are the giving God [Who gives] me wisdom liberally *and* ungrudgingly, without reproaching *or* faultfinding, in the Name of Jesus.

Proverbs 8:12 (AMP) I have God's wisdom and prudence. The wisdom of God is revealing to me witty inventions, to bring me the fullness of my salvation and success today, in the Name of Jesus.

☎ MY MOUTH

Isaiah 49:2 (KJV) God has made my mouth like a sharp sword; in the shadow of His hand hath He hid me, and made me a polished shaft; in His quiver hath He hid me, in the Name of Jesus.

Isaiah 50:4 (KJV) The Lord hath given me the tongue of the learned, that I should know how to speak a word in season to him that is weary: He wakeneth me morning by morning, He wakeneth mine ear to hear as the learned, in the Name of Jesus.

☎ PEACE

1 Peter 5:7 (KJV) Praise God! I refuse to carry the cares of my life and my family's lives. I cast all my cares upon You Lord, for You are caring for us, in the Name of Jesus.

Philippians 4:6-7 (KJV) Father, I have come before You in prayer and supplication with thanksgiving concerning my needs. I am not careful over them, for the peace of God which passeth all understanding is keeping my heart and mind through Christ Jesus, in the Name of Jesus.

Psalm 72:7 (AMP) Glory to God, I am the [uncompromisingly] righteous in His [Christ's] day. I am flourishing and my peace is abounding, till there is a moon no longer, in the Name of Jesus.

Psalm 119:164-165 (AMP) Father, seven times a day *and* all day long do I praise You because of Your righteous decrees. I have great peace because I love Your law; nothing shall offend me or make me stumble, in the Name of Jesus.

John 14:27 (AMP) Lord, thank You for leaving me with peace; Your very [own] peace, You have given and bequeathed to me. Not as the world gives [peace] have You given to me and I will not let my heart be troubled, or let it be afraid. [I have stopped allowing myself to be agitated and disturbed; and I do not permit myself to be fearful and intimidated and cowardly and unsettled], in the Name of Jesus.

Romans 15:33 (AMP) Father, thank You for Your peace. You are my peace giving God and You are with me and my family! Amen (so be it), in the Name of Jesus.

Romans 15:13 (AMP) The God of my hope is filling me with all joy and peace in believing [through the experience of my faith] that by the power of the Holy Spirit, I am abounding and overflowing (bubbling over) with hope, in the Name of Jesus.

☎ PLAN OF GOD

Jeremiah 29:11, 1 Peter 5:7 (MSG) Father, You know what You are doing and You have my life all planned out. You have plans to take care of me, never abandon me and plans to give me the future that I hope for, so I am carefree because You are caring for me, in the Name of Jesus.

Psalm 37:23 (MSG) Praise God! I am delighting in Your ways and You are directing, establishing, and blazing my steps, so I know what steps to take and what to do in every situation, in the Name of Jesus.

Ephesians 3:20 (MSG) Praise the Lord, my God can do anything! I thank You Lord, that You are doing far more than I could ever imagine, guess, or request in my wildest dreams! You've brought this to pass by working within me; Your spirit works deeply and gently within me, in the Name of Jesus.

Psalm 138:8 (BBE) I thank You Lord, that You have perfected everything that concerns me. You are vindicating me, fulfilling Your purpose in me, accomplishing Your plan in me, finishing what You started in me, because Your love and mercy upon me are eternal, in the Name of Jesus.

Psalm 31:19-20 (AMP) Oh, how great is Your goodness, which You have laid up for me, because I fear, revere, and worship You. I see the goodness which You have wrought for me, because I am trusting and taking refuge in You before the sons of men! In the secret place of Your presence, You are hiding me from the plots of men and You are keeping me secretly in Your pavilion from the strife of tongues, in the Name of Jesus.

Joshua 24:15-16 (AMP) It may seem evil to the world to serve the Lord, but as for me and my house, we will serve the Lord, for we say, "Far be it from us to forsake the Lord to serve other gods," in the Name of Jesus.

Colossians 1:9-11 (AMP) Father, I say by faith, that I am filled with the full (deep and clear) knowledge of Your will in all spiritual wisdom [in comprehensive insight into the ways and purposes of You] and in understanding and discernment of spiritual things. I am walking (living and conducting myself) in a manner worthy of You Lord, I am fully pleasing to You and desiring to please You in all things. I am bearing fruit in every good work and steadily growing and increasing in and by the knowledge of You [with fuller, deeper, and clearer insight, acquaintance, and recognition]. Thank You for invigorating and strengthening me with all power according to the might of our glory, [to exercise] every kind of endurance and patience (perseverance and forbearance) with joy, in the Name of Jesus.

☎ PROSPERITY

Malachi 3:10 (KJV) I bring all the tithes into the storehouse, so there will be enough food in God's Temple. Now I believe I receive the promise of God in my life. God is opening up the windows of heaven for me and pouring out "The Blessing." It's so great that I do not have enough room to take it in! I am trying God and He is proving His Word to me, in the Name of Jesus.

Philippians 4:19 (AMP) Thank You Father, for granting my $_____ withdrawal from my heavenly account. I praise You for liberally supplying (filling to the full) my every need according to Your riches in glory in Christ Jesus, in the Name of Jesus.

Deuteronomy 28:12-13 (KJV) Father, I thank You for opening unto me Your good treasure, the heaven to give the rain unto my land and to bless all the work of my hands. I lend to many nations and I do not borrow. I am now the head and not the tail; and I am above only and not beneath, because I am hearkening unto Your commandments, which You command me this day, in the Name of Jesus.

Psalm 66:12 (NLT) Praise God, He has brought me through the fire and flood to my place of great abundance, in the Name of Jesus.

Mark 11:23-24 (KJV) By the power of Your Word, Father I have what I say I have, in the Name of Jesus. According to Your Word Father, I can speak to my life, believing I receive when I pray, with no doubt and the things I say I have will come to pass. Therefore I say, "My monthly income is $_____, I own and drive the best cars, own the best real estate, live in the best homes, acquire the best promotions, own the best businesses, wear the best clothes, I use the best materials and resources in this earth and best of all, I give the best gifts," in the Name of Jesus.

1 Timothy 6:17-18 (AMP) Father, as You commanded, even though I am rich in this world, I am not proud, arrogant and contemptuous of others, nor do I set my hopes on uncertain riches, but on You. For You richly and ceaselessly provide me and my household with everything for [our] enjoyment. I am doing good, being rich in good works, liberal and generous of heart and ready to share [with others], in the Name of Jesus.

Luke 4:19 (AMP) Salvation and the free flavors of God are abounding towards me profusely. Money comes to me through:

1. Multiplied interest & dividends
2. Bill credits and refunds
3. Lost money found
4. Unexpected financial income
5. Financial & Material gifts
6. Bonuses
7. Promotions
8. Jewels & Gems
9. Inheritances
10. Unclaimed money
11. Fee reversals
12. Real Estate
13. Debts Canceled
14. Strangers
15. Profitable Investments
16. _____

Genesis 27:28-29 (AMP) Father, I praise You for giving me and my household the dew of the heavens and of the fatness of the earth and abundance of grain and [new] wine. Thank You for causing people to serve us and nations to bow down to us. You are making us masters in the earth. Everyone who curses us is cursed and favor with blessings is on those who bless us, in the Name of Jesus.

Psalm 31:19 (AMP) Glory to God, Oh how great is Your goodness, which You have laid up for me because I fear, revere and worship You. In You I trust and take refuge before the sons of men, and I am enjoying the goodness that you wrought up for me, in the Name of Jesus.

2 Samuel 23:5 (NLT) Thank You Father! Is it not my family You have chosen? Yes, You have made an everlasting covenant with me. Your agreement is arranged and guaranteed in every detail. You are ensuring me safety and success, in the Name of Jesus.

2 Chronicles 26:4-5 (AMP) Father, I have set myself to seek You all of my days and to follow the instructions of those who are instructing me in the things of You. I believe that as long as I am seeking (inquiring of, yearning for) You Lord, that You [God] are making me to prosper, in the Name of Jesus.

Genesis 39:3 (KJV) Glory to God, all see that God is with me and is making all that I do to flourish and succeed in my hand, in the Name of Jesus.

Ecclesiastes 3:13 (AMP) Thank You for Your great gift Lord. We are eating, drinking and enjoying the good of our labor, in the Name of Jesus.

Proverbs 13:22 (AMP) Father, just as You said, I am good, for I am building and preparing an inheritance [of moral stability and goodness] to my children's children. I receive the wealth of the sinner; [it is finding it's way into my hands], for it was laid up for me, because I am righteous, in the Name of Jesus.

1 Chronicles 17:24 (AMP) Father, let it be established and let Your name [and the character that Your name denotes] be magnified forever, saying, The Lord of hosts, the God of Israel, is my God; and my house will be established before You forever, in the Name of Jesus.

Psalm 92:12-14 (AMP) I am living my life as the [uncompromisingly] righteous and flourishing like the palm tree [I am long-lived, stately, upright, useful, and fruitful]; I am growing like a cedar in Lebanon [majestic, stable, durable, and incorruptible]. I am planted in the house of the Lord, and flourishing in the courts of my God. I am growing in grace and I will still bring forth fruit in old age; because I am full of sap [of spiritual vitality] and [rich in the] verdure [of trust, love, and contentment], in the Name of Jesus.

Proverbs 11:28 (MSG) I am not living the dead life that is devoted to things, but I am living the God-shaped life and my life is a flourishing tree, in the Name of Jesus.

2 Corinthians 9:8 (AMP) Father, I praise You for making all grace (every favor and earthly blessing) come to me and my family in abundance, so that we always and under all circumstances and whatever the need, are self sufficient. We possess enough and require no aid or support. We are furnished in abundance for every good work and charitable donation. Therefore we are able to pay all of our monthly obligations and expenses, with plenty of money left over (after paying our tithes and offerings) because You are providing and multiplying our (resources for) sowing and increasing the fruits of our righteousness (which manifests) itself in active goodness, kindness and charity. We are enriched in all things and in every way, so that we are generous and our generosity brings forth thanksgiving to You Father, in the Name of Jesus.

☎ (SPIRITUAL) GROWTH

Mark 12:30-31 (AMP) I declare that I love the Lord my God, out of and with my whole heart, out of and with all my soul (my life), out of and with all my mind (with my faculty of thought and my moral understanding) and out of and with all my strength. This is the first and principal commandment. And I am also doing the second which is, I love my neighbor as myself, in the Name of Jesus

Psalm 112:1-4 (AMP) Praise the Lord, Hallelujah! We are blessed, happy, fortunate, to be envied because we fear, revere and worship You Lord. We are delighting greatly in Your commandments, and our offspring shall be mighty upon the earth, for the generation of the upright shall be blessed. Prosperity and welfare are in our house, our righteousness is enduring forever and light is arising for us in darkness, because we are upright, gracious, compassionate and just, in the Name of Jesus.

☎ SUCCESS

Ephesians 3:20 (AMP) Father, I glorify and praise You for what you are doing in my life, by (in consequence of) the [action of Your] power that is at work within me. You are [carrying out Your purpose and] doing superabundantly, far over *and* above all that I [dare] ask or think [infinitely beyond my highest prayers, desires, thoughts, hopes, or dreams], in the Name of Jesus.

Luke 1:37 (AMP) Father, all my dreams, goals and visions are coming to pass by the power of Your Word. For with You nothing is ever impossible for me and no Word from You is ever without power or impossible of fulfillment, in the Name of Jesus.

Psalm 2:8 (AMP) Thank You Father, for giving me the nations for my inheritance and the uttermost parts of the earth as my possessions. For by Your power my influence and favor is spreading all over the world, in the Name of Jesus.

Genesis 12:2 (AMP) I praise You Father, for making me [my ministry and business] a great nation and blessing me with an abundant increase of favors. You are making my name famous and distinguished all over the earth and You have made me a blessing, [now I am dispensing good to others], in the Name of Jesus.

Genesis 11:6 (AMP) Father, I imagine [see, and ponder] the great success that You are giving to me. I see the doors of opportunities opening for me because of Your favor, I see the resources I need coming into my hands and I see that I have great influence all over the world. Now, nothing that I have imagined, that I can do is impossible for me, in the Name of Jesus.

Philippians 4:13 (KJV) I am successful because I am doing all things through Christ who is strengthening me, in the Name of Jesus.

John 10:10 (AMP) Father, I glorify You for enabling me to have and enjoy my life. I own and live in a _____ sq. ft. home and I own an abundance of the best real estate in the world. _____ (ministry or business) is one of the most successful ventures of my life, generating astounding revenues. I own the treasures, precious gifts, and the richest commodities of the earth. I own and drive a new _____. I have a $_____ annual income, with additional income streams opening to me frequently. I vacation at the most beautiful locations all over the world.

Thank You Father, for giving me the life of abundance (to the full, till it overflows) and enabling me to give the best gifts, in the Name of Jesus.

Joshua 1:8 (AMP) This Book of the Law is not departing out of my mouth, I am meditating on it day and night observing and doing all that is written in it. Now I am making my way prosperous, dealing wisely and having good success in all that I put my hands to, in the Name of Jesus.

☎ GOD'S WISDOM

2 Corinthians 6:14-16 (AMP) Glory to God, my family and I are not unequally yoked with unbelievers [we do not make mismatched alliances with them or come under a different yoke with them, inconsistent with our faith]. For we understand that there is no partnership between right living and right standing with God, with iniquity and lawlessness. We see that light has no fellowship with darkness. It is clear to us that there is no harmony between Christ and Belial [the devil] nor nothing in common between a believer and an unbeliever, in the Name of Jesus. There can never be agreement between a temple of God and idols. For we are the temple of the living God; even as God said, He is dwelling in and with and among us and walking in and with and among us. He is being our God, and we are being His people. He is being a Father to us as, we are being His sons and daughter, in the Name of Jesus.

James 1:19-20 (AMP) Praise God, we are swift to hear, slow to speak, slow to wrath; for we know the wrath of man worketh not the righteousness of God. Wherefore we have laid apart all filthiness and superfluity of naughtiness, and receiving with meekness the engrafted Word, which is saving our souls, in the Name of Jesus.

Romans 12:1-2 (AMP) Father, I present my body to You a living sacrifice, holy, acceptable, unto God, which is my reasonable service. I am not conformed to this world: but I am being transformed by the renewing of my mind. Now, I am proving what is the good, acceptable and perfect will of God in every area of my life, in the Name of Jesus.

☎ MY PURPOSE

John 4:34 (AMP) Glory to God, my food (nourishment) is to do the will (pleasure) of my Father, and to accomplish and completely finish His work, in the Name Jesus.

John 17:3-4 (AMP) Father, I thank You for giving me eternal life: [it means] I know (perceive, recognize, have become acquainted with, and understand) You, the only true and real God, and [likewise] I know Him, Jesus [as the] Christ (the Anointed One, the Messiah), Whom You have sent. Now I am glorifying You down here on the earth by completing the work that You have given me to do, in the Name of Jesus.

Acts 20:24 (AMP) Nothing of this world moves me, neither do I esteem my life dear to myself, if only I may finish my course with joy and the ministry which I have obtained from [which was entrusted to me by] the Lord Jesus. I am faithfully attesting to the good news (the Gospel) of God's grace (His unmerited favor, spiritual blessing, and mercy), in the Name of Jesus.

☎ REPENTANCE

1 John 1:9 (AMP) Father, I [freely] admit that I have sinned and I confess my sins. Thank You for being faithful and just (true to Your own nature and promises) to forgive me of my sins [dismiss my lawlessness] and [continuously] cleanse me from all unrighteousness [everything that is not in conformity to

Your will in purpose, thought, and action], in the Name of Jesus.

2 Corinthians 7:9-11 (AMP) I give You glory Father, because I am pained into repentance [and I have turned back to You]; for I feel grief such as You mean for me to feel, so that in nothing am I suffering loss through it or harm for what I did. For godly grief and the pain that You have been permitted to direct in me, has produced a repentance that is leading and contributing to my salvation and deliverance from evil, that will never bring regret. I do not have the worldly grief (the hopeless sorrow that is characteristic of the pagan world) which is deadly [breeding and ending in death]. For I can see what this same godly sorrow has done for me *and* produced in me. I have an eagerness *and* earnest care to explain *and* clear myself [of all complicity in the condoning of _____ (the sin). I am filled with indignation [at the sin], alarm, yearning, zeal to do justice to all concerned. I am ready to mete out punishment [to the offender, *Satan*]! At every point I am proving myself cleared *and* guiltless in the matter, in the Name of Jesus.

☎ REAL ESTATE OWNERSHIP

Deuteronomy 33:23 (KJV) Glory to God, by the power of Deuteronomy 33:23, just as Naphtali, I am satisfied with favour and I am full of the Blessing of the Lord; possessing the west and the south, in the Name of Jesus.

Deuteronomy 6:10-12 (AMP) Thank You Father, for ushering me and my family into the land You swore to our fathers: Abraham, Isaac, and Jacob, to give us. We are walking into large, bustling cities we didn't build, we own well-furnished houses we didn't buy. You've given us wells we didn't dig, vineyards and olive orchards we didn't plant. Now that we are taking it all in, and we have settled down, pleased and content; we are making sure not to forget how we got here. You, our God, brought us out of slavery in Egypt, (to our enemies) we will always deeply respect You,

Father, in the Name of Jesus.

Isaiah 32:18 (AMP) By the power of God, my family and I own and live in homes and dwelling places that are peaceable habitations, safe dwellings, and quiet resting places, in the Name of Jesus.

Isaiah 65:21-23 (AMP) Praise God forever, we are building houses and inhabiting them, and we are planting vineyards and eating the fruit of them. We are not building and having another (take them and) inhabit; we are not planting to have another eat [the fruit]. For as the days of a tree, so shall our days be as the people of God. We are the chosen and elect of God, making long use of and enjoying the work of our hands. All our labors are not in vain and we are not bringing forth our [children] for sudden terror or calamity; for they are our descendants, the blessed of the Lord, and their offspring shall also be with them, in the Name of Jesus.

☎ RIGHTEOUSNESS

1 Corinthians 15:34 (KJV) I am awake to righteousness, and I sin not; as some who have not the knowledge of God, in the Name of Jesus.

2 Corinthians 5:21 (KJV) He hath made Jesus to be sin for me, who knew no sin; now I am the righteousness of God in Him, in the Name of Jesus.

Ephesians 4:24-25 (AMP) I am constantly renewed in the spirit of my mind [having a fresh mental and spiritual attitude] and I am putting on a new nature (the regenerate self) created in God's image, [Godlike] in true righteousness and holiness, in the Name of Jesus.

Matthew 6:33 (AMP) I am seeking (aiming at and striving after) first of all God's kingdom and His righteousness, His way of doing and being right), and now all these things taken together are being given to me, in the Name of Jesus.

Genesis 1:26 (AMP) Father just as You said, You have made me in Your image, after Your likeness. Now I have complete authority over the fish of the sea, the birds of the air, the [tame] beasts, over all of the earth, and over everything that creeps upon the earth, in the Name of Jesus.

2 Corinthians 5:17-18 (KJV) I am in Christ, and I am a new creature; old things are passed away, behold, all things have become new. All things are from God, who has reconciled me to Himself by Jesus Christ, and has given to me the ministry of reconciliation, in the Name of Jesus.

Romans 5:17 (KJV) Father, I receive the abundance of grace and the gift of righteousness to reign in this life, through the One, Jesus Christ, in the Name of Jesus.

☎ SELF CONFIDENCE

Psalm 139:13-15 (MSG*)* Oh yes Father, You shaped me first inside, then out; You formed me in my mother's womb. I thank You, High God—You are breathtaking! Body and soul, I am marvelously made! I worship You in adoration, for what a creation You have made me! You know me inside and out, You know every bone in my body; You know exactly how I was made, bit by bit, how I was sculpted from nothing into something, in the Name of Jesus.

2 Corinthians 10:17-18 (AMP) Father, I make my boasts and glories boast in the Lord. For it is not by praising and commending myself that I am approved and accepted, but it is because You have accredited and commended me, in the Name of Jesus.

☎ VICTORY

Isaiah 54:17 (AMP) Praise God, no weapon that is formed against my family and I shall prosper, and every tongue that arises against us in judgment, we show to be in the wrong. This [peace, righteousness, security, triumph over opposition] is our heritage as the servants of the Lord [we are those in whom the ideal Servant of the Lord is reproduced]; this is the righteousness or the vindication which we have obtain from the Lord [this is that which the Lord has imparted to us as our justification], in the Name of Jesus.

Psalm 44:4-7 (AMP) Father, You are my King, Who commands victories and deliverance for me and my family. Through You we push down our enemies, through Your Name we tread down under all who rise up against us. For I will not trust in and lean on my bow, neither shall my sword save me. But You have saved us from our foes and have put them to shame who hate us, in the Name of Jesus.

Psalm 62:6-7 (AMP) God only is my Rock and my Salvation; He is my Defense and my Fortress, I shall not be moved. With God rests my salvation and my glory; He is my Rock of unyielding strength and impenetrable hardness, and my refuge is in God, in the Name of Jesus.

Psalm 118:14-15 (AMP) The Lord is my Strength and Song; and He has become my Salvation. My voice is full of rejoicing and salvation in my tents *and* private dwellings, because I am one of the [uncompromisingly] righteous: the right hand of the Lord does valiantly *and* achieves strength for me, in the Name of Jesus.

John 14:1 (AMP) I will not let my heart be troubled distressed, agitated). I am believing in, adhering to, trusting in and relying on God; I am also believing in, adhering to, trusting in, and relying on the Lord, in the Name of Jesus.

Exodus 14:13-14 (AMP) Just as Moses told the people FEAR NOT, I will NOT FEAR; I am standing still (firm, confident, undismayed) and I will see the salvation of the Lord, which He has worked for me today. For the Egyptians (the enemies) I have seen today, I will never see again. For the Lord is fighting for me, and I am holding my peace and remaining at rest, in the Name of Jesus.

Job 5:20-22 (AMP) Glory to God, in famine You have redeemed us from death, and in war from the power of the sword. We are hidden from the scourge of the tongue, neither are we afraid of destruction. For through You Father, at destruction and famine we shall laugh, neither are we afraid of the living creatures of the earth, in the Name of Jesus.

Nehemiah 8:10 (AMP) Praise God, we are going our way, eating the fat, drinking the sweet drink, and sending portions to him for whom nothing is prepared; for this day is holy to You, our Lord. We are not grieved and depressed, for the joy of the Lord is our strength and stronghold, in the Name Jesus.

☎ UNSAVED LOVED ONES

Acts 16:31 (AMP) Thank You Father, for saving me and all of my household because, I believe in the Lord Jesus Christ. That is, I have taken myself out of my own keeping and I have entrusted myself and my family to Your keeping, in the Name of Jesus.

John 1:41 (AMP) In the Name of Jesus, I am seeking after and finding my own family members to tell them, I have found (discovered) the Messiah!—which translated is the Christ (the Anointed One). Then, I am leading them to Jesus.

☎ WEIGHT LOSS

Galatians 5:24 (AMP) Glory to God, I belong to Christ Jesus (the Messiah) and I have crucified my flesh (the godless human nature) with it's passions and appetites and desires. Now, I have complete control over my passions, appetites and desires, therefore I do not overeat, in the Name of Jesus.

Proverbs 23:2-3 (AMP) In the Name of Jesus, I put a knife to my throat when I am tempted to be given to desire. I am not desirous of his dainties, for it is a deceitful food (offered with questionable motives).

Proverbs 25:27 (AMP) By the power of God, I do not eat too much honey; nor do I seek the glory of men for my own glory; for I know that this causes suffering and is not glory, in the Name of Jesus.

Proverbs 25:16 (AMP) When I find [pleasure sweet like] honey, I only eat as much as is sufficient for myself. I refuse to be filled with it until I vomit, in the Name of Jesus.

Mark 11:23-24 (AMP) According to Your Word Father, I can speak to my body, believing I receive when I pray, with no doubt and those things will come to pass in my body. Therefore I speak to my body and I say, "Metabolism you are actively burning all excess fat in my body, to the perfect weight of _____lbs. and my waist is _____ inches. Body, you are not storing any excess fat cells any where. You are healthy, strong and physically fit in every aspect of the Word of God. All your clothes look fabulous on you, with no bulging or protruding fat rolls anywhere. You only eat when you are hungry and stop when you are politely full. I keep you under submission to me at all times, making you my slave and you never overeat. Now you are glorifying God in strength, discipline, and appearance," in the Name of Jesus.

Forever Oh Lord, Your Word Is Settled In Heaven, Of Which I Am a Citizen Of, In the Name of Jesus.

Ezekiel 36:26-28 (AMP)

A new heart will I give you and a new spirit will I put within you, and I will take away the stony heart out of your flesh and give you a heart of flesh. And I will put my Spirit within you and cause you to walk in My statutes, and you shall heed My ordinances and do them. And you shall dwell in the land that I gave to your fathers; and you shall be My people, and I will be your God.

Meditation:

The Lord has given me a new heart and put a new spirit within me. He has taken out the stony heart and now I have a heart of flesh. He has put His Spirit within me and He is causing me to walk in His statutes. I am heeding His ordinances and doing them. Now, I am dwelling in the land that the Lord gave to my fathers, for I am His and He is my God, in the Name of Jesus.

I Am No Longer Conformed To This World. I Am Being Transformed By the Renewing Of My Mind, in the Name of Jesus.

Writing Your Own Personalized Prayers

WRITING YOUR OWN PERSONALIZED PRAYERS

Writing your own personalized prayers, is an exercise that every Believer should be doing. No matter what issues you may face in life, the Word of God has the answer to address every situation. Go to the Word of God and get the promises that apply to that area (two or three Scriptures) and use this section to write them out, in first person present-tense (similar to what was done in the Personalized Prayer section). Begin to proclaim these prayers every day.

Writing out your own personalized prayers, helps to build your faith by seeing the promise of God that specifically addresses your need. When Satan comes with lies to try to distract and discourage you, that is the perfect time to confess these personalized prayers. They will build your faith, keep you on track, remind you of what God says, and refocus you.

God bless you as you create God's wondrous plan for your life.

Pastor Sandy

WRITING YOUR OWN PERSONALIZED PRAYERS

WRITE YOUR OWN PRAYERS. (REMEMBER TO PERSONALIZE THE SCRIPTURE IN PRESENT TENSE).

_____

_____

_____

_____

_____

_____

_____

_____

_____

_____

_____

_____

_____

_____

_____

_____

_____

_____

_____

_____

_____

_____

_____

_____

_____

_____

_____

_____

_____

_____

WRITING YOUR OWN PERSONALIZED PRAYERS

WRITE YOUR OWN PRAYERS. (REMEMBER TO PERSONALIZE THE SCRIPTURE IN PRESENT TENSE).

WRITING YOUR OWN PERSONALIZED PRAYERS

WRITE YOUR OWN PRAYERS. (REMEMBER TO PERSONALIZE THE SCRIPTURE IN PRESENT TENSE).

_____
_____
_____
_____
_____
_____
_____
_____
_____
_____
_____
_____
_____
_____
_____
_____
_____
_____
_____
_____
_____
_____
_____
_____
_____
_____
_____
_____
_____
_____

WRITING YOUR OWN PERSONALIZED PRAYERS

WRITE YOUR OWN PRAYERS. (REMEMBER TO PERSONALIZE THE SCRIPTURE IN PRESENT TENSE).

WRITING YOUR OWN PERSONALIZED PRAYERS

WRITE YOUR OWN PRAYERS. (REMEMBER TO PERSONALIZE THE SCRIPTURE IN PRESENT TENSE).

_____

_____

_____

_____

_____

_____

_____

_____

_____

_____

_____

_____

_____

_____

_____

_____

_____

_____

_____

_____

_____

_____

_____

_____

_____

_____

_____

_____

_____

1 Thessalonians 5:23 (AMP)

And may the God of peace Himself sanctify you through and through [separate you from profane things, make you pure and wholly consecrated to God]; and may your spirit and soul and body be preserved sound and complete [and found] blameless at the coming of our Lord Jesus Christ (the Messiah).

Meditation:

The God of all peace is Himself sanctifying me through and through [separating me from profane things, making me pure and wholly consecrated to Him]. I decree by faith, that my spirit, soul and body are being preserved sound and complete [and found] blameless at the coming of my Lord Jesus Christ (the Messiah), in the Name of Jesus.

I Am Mediating the Word Of God Day And Night. I See How To Make My Way Prosperous, in the Name of Jesus.

Revelation From God

Revelation From God

Keeping track of the revelation God gives you is essential to creating His perfect plan for your life (Eph. 3:17-18 KJV). He sees and knows what we do not see and know, so when He reveals instructions or wisdom to you, do not just forget about it. You need to write it down and read it frequently. It is your next step to success.

This section will assist you in keeping track of the revelation God gives you. Being diligent about this, will also be the very key to developing your daily walk and relationship with the Lord.

Obeying His instructions and believing His encouraging Words are all part of cultivating your relationship with Him.

Write down what you hear Him say, then judge the accuracy of what you hear by Scripture. Remember, He will never speak contrary to Scripture.

God Bless!
Pastor Sandy

<u>Revelation From God</u>

Date_____

_____
_____
_____
_____
_____
_____
_____
_____
_____
_____
_____
_____
_____

Date_____

_____
_____
_____
_____
_____
_____
_____
_____
_____
_____
_____
_____
_____
_____

Revelation From God

Date_____

_____
_____
_____
_____
_____
_____
_____
_____
_____
_____
_____
_____

Date_____

_____
_____
_____
_____
_____
_____
_____
_____
_____
_____
_____
_____

REVELATION FROM GOD

Date_____

_____
_____
_____
_____
_____
_____
_____
_____
_____
_____
_____

Date_____

_____
_____
_____
_____
_____
_____
_____
_____
_____
_____
_____
_____
_____

REVELATION FROM GOD

Date_____

_____
_____
_____
_____
_____
_____
_____
_____
_____
_____
_____
_____

Date_____

_____
_____
_____
_____
_____
_____
_____
_____
_____
_____
_____
_____
_____

Revelation From God

Date_____

_____
_____
_____
_____
_____
_____
_____
_____
_____
_____
_____
_____

Date_____

_____
_____
_____
_____
_____
_____
_____
_____
_____
_____
_____
_____
_____
_____
_____

REVELATION FROM GOD

Date_____

_____
_____
_____
_____
_____
_____
_____
_____
_____
_____
_____
_____

Date_____

_____
_____
_____
_____
_____
_____
_____
_____
_____
_____
_____
_____
_____

REVELATION FROM GOD

Date_____

_____
_____
_____
_____
_____
_____
_____
_____
_____
_____
_____
_____

Date_____

_____
_____
_____
_____
_____
_____
_____
_____
_____
_____
_____
_____
_____
_____

Revelation From God

Date_____

_____

_____

_____

_____

_____

_____

_____

_____

_____

_____

_____

_____

Date_____

_____

_____

_____

_____

_____

_____

_____

_____

_____

_____

_____

_____

_____

Revelation From God

Date_____

_____

_____

_____

_____

_____

_____

_____

_____

_____

_____

_____

_____

Date_____

_____

_____

_____

_____

_____

_____

_____

_____

_____

_____

_____

_____

_____

Job 32:8 (AMP)

But there is [a vital force] a spirit [of intelligence] in man, and the breath of the Almighty gives men understanding.

Meditation:

But there is [a vital force] a spirit [of intelligence] in me, and the breath of the Almighty is giving me understanding. All the answers to the issues and questions in my life are rising up in me from the breath of the Almighty, in the Name of Jesus.

Not One Word Of God Has Fallen To The Ground Void Of Power. Every Word Has Prospered & Done Exactly What God Said It Would Do.

Answered Prayers

Answered Prayers *(Write them down)*

Date_____

Praise Report_____

_____

_____

_____

_____

Date_____

Praise Report_____

_____

_____

_____

_____

Date_____

Praise Report_____

_____

_____

_____

_____

ANSWERED PRAYERS *(WRITE THEM DOWN)*

Date_____

Praise Report_____

_____

_____

_____

_____

Date_____

Praise Report_____

_____

_____

_____

_____

Date_____

Praise Report_____

_____

_____

_____

_____

ANSWERED PRAYERS *(WRITE THEM DOWN)*

Date_____

Praise Report_____

_____

_____

_____

_____

Date_____

Praise Report_____

_____

_____

_____

_____

Date_____

Praise Report_____

_____

_____

_____

_____

ANSWERED PRAYERS *(WRITE THEM DOWN)*

Date_____

Praise Report_____

_____

_____

_____

_____

Date_____

Praise Report_____

_____

_____

_____

_____

Date_____

Praise Report_____

_____

_____

_____

_____

ANSWERED PRAYERS *(WRITE THEM DOWN)*

Date_____

Praise Report_____

_____

_____

_____

_____

Date_____

Praise Report_____

_____

_____

_____

_____

Date_____

Praise Report_____

_____

_____

_____

_____

ANSWERED PRAYERS *(WRITE THEM DOWN)*

Date_____

Praise Report_____

_____

_____

_____

_____

Date_____

Praise Report_____

_____

_____

_____

_____

Date_____

Praise Report_____

_____

_____

_____

_____

ANSWERED PRAYERS *(WRITE THEM DOWN)*

Date_____

Praise Report_____

_____

_____

_____

_____

Date_____

Praise Report_____

_____

_____

_____

_____

Date_____

Praise Report_____

_____

_____

_____

_____

ANSWERED PRAYERS *(WRITE THEM DOWN)*

Date_____

Praise Report_____

_____

_____

_____

_____

Date_____

Praise Report_____

_____

_____

_____

_____

Date_____

Praise Report_____

_____

_____

_____

_____

ANSWERED PRAYERS *(WRITE THEM DOWN)*

Date_____

Praise Report_____

_____

_____

_____

_____

Date_____

Praise Report_____

_____

_____

_____

_____

Date_____

Praise Report_____

_____

_____

_____

_____

PRAYER GUIDE REORDER FORM

Name _____

Address _____

City _____ State _____

Zip Code _____ Telephone _____

Signature _____

Qty	Item Description	Price each	Total
	Will You Answer the Call To Pray?	$20.00	

SHIPPING COST	SUBTOTAL	
IN THE USA ADD $5.95	SALES TAX	
OUTSIDE THE USA $8.95	OFFERING	
SHIPPING & HANDLING	SHIPPING	
	TOTAL ENCLOSED	

PLEASE ALLOW 2 TO 4 WEEKS FOR DELIVERY.

RETURN POLICY: SANDY MAYS MINISTRIES WILL REPLACE ANY DEFECTIVE MERCHANDISE WITHIN THE FIRST 30 DAYS OF PURCHASE.

Include check or money order and mail with order form to:
Sandy Mays Ministries
5575 Simmons #1-365
North Las Vegas, NV. 89031
(702) 364-9041
Or visit: www.pastorsandy.org

You can also order directly from the Book Store at www.pubgraphicsdirect.com

If you have a prayer request, please include it here:

_____

_____

_____

_____

_____

_____

_____

_____

_____

_____

_____

_____

_____

_____

I would like to become a ministry partner with Sandy Mays Ministries.

Our commitment to you as a partner is to...
1. Pray for you on a daily basis.
2. Periodically supply you with newsletters and other teaching publications to encourage and strengthen your faith.

Your commitment to us as a partner is to...
1. Pray for us always.
2. Support us financially with your monthly pledge.
   "Not because I desire a gift; but I desire fruit that may abound to your account." Phil. 4:17

Name_____

Address_____

City_____ State_____

Zip code_____ Telephone # _____

Dear Sandy, Yes, I want to make a commitment to become a monthly financial and prayer supporter. I commit to a monthly gift of:

___$10 ___$20 ___$25 ___$35 ___$50 ___$100

I have enclosed a one time gift of: $_____

Reverend Sandy Mays is the founder of Las Vegas Church of the Harvest, located in Las Vegas, Nevada. A non-denomination, multi-racial Body of Believer's, where she teaches on love, application and meditation of the Word of God. Her ministry is inspiring Christians all over the world to experience the life changing power that comes with applying of the Word of God.

In 2012, Pastor Sandy founded Harvest Radio Network, a 24 hours 7 days a week internet radio network that is boosting faith should be all over the globe (www.harvestradionetwork.org). She has also authored other mind renewal materials that equip Believers to see themselves the way that God sees them and live a life of victory, appropriating the Word of God.

For more information visit: www.lvchonline.org or call
702-364-9041